ART OF THE WESTERN WORLD

DUTCH PAINTING

PETER MITCHELL

PAUL HAMLYN · LONDON

ART OF THE WESTERN WORLD

General Editor Marco Valsecchi

DUTCH PAINTING

The paintings in this volume are reproduced by permission of
the Istituto Geografico De Agostini, Novara (Plates 2, 4, 5, 11, 20, 23)
Arborio Mella, Milan (Plates 1, 21), Kempter, Munich (Plate 7)
the Rijksmuseum, Amsterdam (Plates 3, 8, 9, 12, 13, 14, 16, 17, 18, 19, 22, 24)
Scala, Florence (Plates 6, 10, 15)

The selection of the paintings was made by Professor Luigi Mallé,
Curator of the Civic Museum, Turin.

Printed in Italy by Istituto Geografico De Agostini - Novara - 1965

INTRODUCTION

The most obvious, if not the most remarkable, thing about Dutch painting is the shortness of its history as an important European school. The 'Golden Age' of Dutch art lasted barely seventy years, from about 1610 to about 1680. Before that, the art of the region now called Holland (the modern state of the Netherlands) had been little more than a branch of the German, Burgundian or Flemish schools, though some specifically Dutch qualities had begun to emerge during the fifteenth and sixteenth centuries. After the Golden Age was over, Holland once more became an artistic backwater. It was not until the later nineteenth century that another great artist of Dutch origin appeared : Van Gogh. But Van Gogh, and still more his twentieth-century successors, must be classed with the international movement in modern art rather than with the Dutch School proper.

Yet if Dutch painting properly so-called was a short-lived phenomenon, it was amazingly rich both in quantity and quality of achievement. A nation that produced Rembrandt, Frans Hals, Vermeer, Van Goyen, Cuyp, Seghers, Ruisdael, Terbrugghen, Terborch and Jan Steen—to say nothing of innumerable lesser masters—is one of the major artistic nations of Europe by virtue of that fact alone, irrespective of whether it all took place within a single century. Perhaps only the Italian and French schools have been still more productive of great masterpieces. It is therefore with the art of the seventeenth century, rather than with earlier or later periods, that this book is almost exclusively concerned.

But first, how did this Dutch 'Renaissance' come about? Why in Holland? Why did it begin only in the seventeenth century and not earlier? And why was there then a decline? It goes without saying that nothing can explain the appearance of artistic genius as such. Nevertheless, the rise of Dutch painting does seem to be more readily explicable in terms of outside factors—historical, religious and social—than that of most other European schools. If these factors did not *produce* the art (as they certainly did not), they provided a stimulus and a setting in which that art could flourish. They also helped to determine its character.

The Dutch effectively became an independent nation in 1609. During the two previous centuries, both the Northern Netherlands (Holland) and the Southern Netherlands (Flanders) had belonged to foreign powers: first Burgundy, then the Holy Roman Empire, and finally—from the mid-sixteenth century onwards—Spain. Dutch independence was gained only after a long war of rebellion against the Spanish occupying forces — a war that was religious as well as nationalistic in character, since the Dutch had adopted the Protestant faith. Eventually, in 1609, the two sides agreed to a truce, the advantages from which lay mostly with the Dutch. Commerce prospered, a great navy was built, colonies were established overseas, and by the mid-seventeenth century Amsterdam had replaced the Flemish city of Antwerp as the chief port in Northern Europe. Although fighting was resumed in 1621, the Dutch more than held their own, and at the general European settlement of 1648 which ended the Thirty Years War, Holland was internationally recognised as a fully sovereign federation of states—the 'United Provinces'. Technically Holland is the name for only one of these provinces and not for the country as a whole, though Holland is itself the largest of the provinces. But modern English usage sanctions the word 'Holland' for the whole country and this word is used throughout the present book in order to avoid confusion.

The chief sources of power in the state were the city merchants, or burghers, the clergy, and the Stadholder (Governor-General). Of these three, the merchants were undoubtedly the strongest. Their energy and wealth brought prosperity not only to themselves but also to the nation at large. Indeed, it is a remarkable thing that all except the poorest classes seem to have shared in the intense commercial activity of the age. Even art was treated as a commodity and was bought and sold on the open market. "We arrived late at Roterdam," wrote the English diarist, John Evelyn, in 1641, "where was at that time their annual Mart or Faire, so furnish'd with pictures (especially Landscips and Drolleries, as they call those clownish representations) as I was amaz'd: '...tis an ordinary thing to find a common Farmor lay out two, or 3000 pounds in this Commodity, their houses are full of them, and they vend them at their Kermas'es village festivals to very greate gaines." Painters were among the most avid collectors of their colleagues' work.

The subject matter of art was chiefly taken from the environment of the people themselves: their streets, houses, churches, countryside; their sea-coast, rivers and canals; the food they ate, the flowers and fruit they grew; above all, their own way of life, whether 'popular' or bourgeois. It followed that portraiture flourished too. There was comparatively little demand for religious or mythological art and churches were almost bare of decoration. Yet it must not be supposed that all religious subjects were forbidden or that Catholicism was totally suppressed. Despite occasional persecution, Catholics were generally allowed to hold Masses in private and the city of Utrecht actually had a Catholic majority among its population. More than this, one of the staunchest Protestants and the greatest Dutch painter of the century—Rembrandt van Rijn—turned again and again to the Bible for the material of his art. Indeed, Rembrandt confounds generalisations on this as on almost every other aspect of Dutch painting one can think of. For instance, whereas most of his contemporaries were specialists in one genre or another, he took all types of subject matter as his province. He was at once the most Dutch, and the most universal, painter of his age. By virtue of his colossal eminence he dominated seventeenth-century Dutch painting, yet he was also in a sense detached and isolated from it.

In view of their (sometimes fanatical) Protestantism, the clergy played a mainly negative role in the patronage of painting, but the Stadholder, whose power balanced that of the city merchants, encouraged a limited kind of court art. In fact, the Stadholdership, which had become hereditary in the House of Orange, had many of the attributes of a monarchy; both William II and William III married English princesses and in 1688 William III succeeded to the English throne. Under the civilised and able Prince Frederick-Henry (1584-1647), a more cosmopolitan style than any to be found elsewhere was established at The Hague. Other cities also produced distinctive styles of their own, although the short distances between them led to frequent movement and exchange of influence. Utrecht, for example, was noted for the Italianate tendencies of its art, both in landscape and figure painting. A tradition of meticulously detailed brushwork became associated with Leyden. Delft painting can be recognised by its refined, bourgeois character and by the use of a special kind of blue pigment. Amsterdam was the home of a grander, more masculine, type of bourgeois art and was also the home of Rembrandt for the greater part of his life. And so on. Despite an overall consistency in Dutch painting—a consistency reflected in the appearance of style changes in all fields at once, whether landscape, genre, portraiture or still life—it is remarkable how often regional differences remain clear. To some extent this was due to the federal character of the Dutch constitution and to the way in which the cities clung to their ancient rights and privileges.

In a brief review such as this, the fifteenth and sixteenth centuries must be passed over rapidly. The most notable 'Dutch' artist of the fifteenth century was the gentle and charming Geertgen tot Sint Jans (about 1460 to about 1490), who probably worked in Leyden or Haarlem and who was a sort of equivalent to the Fleming, Dirk Bouts. In the next generation styles changed in accordance with Flemish and German developments and, a little later, as a result of Italian influences as well. The chief figure during this period was Lucas van Leyden (?1494-1533), an artist better known for his woodcuts and engravings than for his paintings. He was much influenced by Dürer and worked in Flanders for part of his life. He was followed by Jan van Scorel (1495-1562) and Marten van Heemskerk (1498-1574), both of whom visited Italy and were affected by Italian fashions. Mannerism took root, especially in Heemskerk's work. In an effort to combat this, an academy of painting was founded at Haarlem in the 1580's by the 'Dutch Vasari', Karel van Mander (1548-1606). However, the impulse behind this academy was still Italian and the gains in the direction of realism—the introduction of more natural figure proportions, a more rational treatment of space, greater compositional clarity, and so on—were strictly limited. It should also be noted that the links between Dutch and Flemish painting at this period remained strong and that the way in which a native school of Dutch painting initally evolved was through the emigration of Flemish-born artists, who left their home towns for the north as a result of Spanish persecution. One such artist was the first great master of Dutch painting: Frans Hals.

Hals' family had settled in Haarlem by the time he was ten (in 1591) and partly because of his presence there, partly because of the prestige of the academy, this city was the liveliest centre of painting in Holland during the first quarter of the seventeenth century. It was incidentally the third largest in size after Amsterdam and Leyden, and was the scene of the first experiments in realistic genre and landscape painting. Hals' genius put an unmistakable stamp on Haarlem art. His style was vigorous, forceful and extrovert, and these qualities were communicated not only to younger Haarlem painters, such as Berchem and Wouwermans, but also to painters from other cities who settled in Haarlem for part of their lives—for example Jan Steen. The Flemish genre painter, Adriaen Brouwer, also spent part of his career in Haarlem, where he was

certainly in touch with Hals and may have worked for a short time in the latter's studio. Ostade, Brouwer's successor as the leading Dutch painter of peasant genre, was a gentler spirit but he shared the typical Haarlem directness in his treatment of subject matter.

Another side to Haarlem painting is represented by the landscape painters, Cornelis Vroom and Salomon van Ruysdael; the still-life painter, W. C. Heda; and further, the most remarkable Dutch painter of church interiors, Pieter Saenredam. All four were born in or slightly before 1600 and by the 1630's had developed a calm, simple, almost monochrome style of great poetic beauty. It is with these artists—and, of course, with others of the same generation in other cities—that we reach the phase known as 'tone painting'. Local colours, and even forms, tend to be subordinated to an overall effect of atmosphere and subtly modulated shades of grey, grey-green or brown. Compositions are reduced to a single, simple motif: the transept of a church, a stretch of river, a sand-dune, a farmhouse by a country road, a glass of wine on a table with a pipe and a half-peeled lemon. Then, with the early work of Jacob Ruisdael (dating from just before 1650), colour and plasticity of form return. But Ruisdael, though born and trained in Haarlem, later moved to Amsterdam. A tendency for painters to converge on Amsterdam became common in the second half of the century.

Two other centres besides Haarlem were of importance in the 1610's and 1620's: Utrecht and The Hague. Utrecht was, as has already been said, the chief focus of Italian influence in the seventeenth century, and most Utrecht painters spent a period of study in Rome. The model for the figure painters, Honthorst, Terbrugghen and Baburen, was the art of Caravaggio: his subject matter, his liking for bold compositions and theatrical clothes, his use of strong colours and sharp contrasts of light and shade. His Dutch followers in fact modified his style fairly rapidly and gave it a softer, more lyrical quality which was later transmitted to Vermeer. The landscape painters, on the other hand, attached themselves to the ideal landscape tradition, and those who returned from Rome after 1640 (for example, Jan Both) brought back a style inspired by Claude Lorrain.

At The Hague it was Flemish influence rather than Italian which predominated. This can be seen in the court portraits painted there by Honthorst (who moved to The Hague in the 1630's) and in the painted decorations of the hunting lodge known as the Huis ten Bosch (House in the Wood). Here, Flemish followers of Rubens collaborated with Honthorst and other Dutch artists to produce a series of allegorical compositions in honour of the Stadholder and his family that was a sort of provincial equivalent of Rubens' Marie de Médicis cycle for the Palais du Luxembourg. To turn to a very different kind of art, The Hague was also the home of the landscape painter Jan van Goyen for much of his life. Van Goyen was, indeed, the greatest master of 'tonal' landscapes in seventeenth-century Dutch art. In the 1640's he brought the depiction of the flat Dutch countryside, with its dunes and estuaries and high, cloud-filled skies, to a pitch of calm, almost classic, perfection. Within certain limits— the lack of colour, the lack of movement, the lack of formal complexity—an extraordinary degree of realism was now achieved. The same was true in marine painting, still-life painting, portraiture and, with reservations, genre. It was a realism that owed nothing to either Italian or Flemish example. It was wholly Dutch.

At Amsterdam a tradition of fine portrait painting had existed since the later sixteenth century. In the early seventeenth century, Thomas de Keyser (1596/7-1667) was the outstanding figure among a group of portraitists. The city was a rich trading centre where an increasing number of wealthy private patrons was available, apart from the many institutions and societies which regularly had their members portrayed singly or as a group. In 1632 came strong competition for portrait commissions in the shape of Rembrandt Harmensz. van Rijn.

In a brief survey of Dutch painting, an attempt can hardly be made to give a detailed account of Rembrandt's career and the nature of his art, when a small library of books has already been written in such an attempt. Nonetheless, a considerable proportion of available space must be devoted to Rembrandt, not only because of his own achievements, but because of his enormous influence on all forms of Dutch painting in the seventeenth century, which is, in turn, only one aspect of his great importance in the history of painting. It is perhaps unfortunate that whenever the world is blessed with a genius, he seems too busy to write his memoirs or any

letters about himself, or else the task is beyond him. What facts are known about the personality and character of men like Cervantes, Shakespeare and Rembrandt would scarcely cover a few pages. The answer is thought to lie in their works. Naturally, the interpretation of the work of a genius by later nongeniuses leaves room for considerable doubt and diversity of opinion. In my view, genius is an inborn quality which keeps its fascination by remaining a partially solved mystery.

Rembrandt was born in Leyden in 1606, the son of a miller, and full of robust health and energy. In 1620 he made a brief appearance at the Latin School at Leyden but soon devoted himself to becoming a painter. His education came from having the Bible, with all its absorbing stories, read to him from an early age, as was the common practice. He must have had a curious and observant eye and felt very strongly the fascination that the very old have for the very young. Proof of his inquisitive nature is shown by his indeatigable powers as a draughtsman throughout his life. His period of apprenticeship was from 1620-1624, which saw the largely unaided development of his own natural abilities. The most important influence was that of Pieter Lastman (1583-1633) with whom Rembrandt spent six months in Amsterdam, before returning to Leyden, where he worked until his final move to Amsterdam. Although his early Biblical stories clearly show the influence of Lastman, just as his early portraits show the influence of de Keyser, it was the artificial lighting of Caravaggio which attracted Rembrandt. He realised that it could be made to give drama and mystery to the ancient Bible stories. At first, he used extreme contrasts of bright light against darkness, as in the little panel of *The Flight into Egypt* (Tours, Museum). Perfection in the rendering of the properties of light, and then employing it for every variety of artistic purpose, occupies a key position in Rembrandt's development. Together with this early desire to paint his own visions of the Biblical stories came a strong interest in portrait painting, on which his reputation and income in the early years at Amsterdam depended. As a young unknown artist he found that the easiest face to study was his own, or the faces of his family. The essentially introvert side of his nature made him continually portray himself throughout his life. His sixty-odd self portraits are an amazing pictorial autobiography but one should not try to relate too closely the expressions of the portraits with the events of his life. Thus two main interests, Biblical stories and portraiture, emerged at the very beginning of his career and remained his preoccupations until the end of his life. The two subjects have a common basis. Rembrandt realised that the human face could be portrayed to show not only an exacting physical likeness but also what was revealed there of the mind of the sitter. He was absorbed both in the study of the individual face and in the problems and emotions of human life itself. He began to see the Bible stories, not as ancient tales, but as timeless examples of Man's troubled existence, embracing all human emotions. Rembrandt's singular preoccupation with human life and the human soul makes him the most sympathetic and easily understood of all great artists.

As a young man, he must have taken an intelligent interest in the many available examples of the art of other schools, but relied mainly on his own instinct and inventive powers. No clearer proof could be given of his inventive genius and ability to handle paint than *The Anatomy Lesson of Dr Tulp* (1632, The Hague, Mauritshuis). Here was a new conception of the group portrait. Each face is exactly portrayed yet the whole group is united by the concentration of interest on a single focal point. To the spectator there is not so much the feeling of looking at a group as of being present, himself, at a rare and important event. The tonality is actually cool throughout, but how warm it seems compared to the grey-greenish white of the corpse! It satisfied the patrons, not only as a portrait, but because it had captured the drama and dignity of the profession. All this was the work of a man of 26.

The *Anatomy Lesson* opened a decade of material success. The following year, Prince Frederick Henry, on the advice of Huygens, commissioned a Passion Series now in Munich. Rembrandt's marriage to Saskia van Uylenburgh was a happy advance in his fortunes. He was able to give vent to his strong collector's instinct by buying paintings, exotic clothes and all kinds of artistic paraphernalia. He enjoyed painting Saskia, clad in these jewels and rich clothes with their sparkle and textures. Pupils gathered round him whom he taught patiently but without disturbing his own prodigious output. In 1639 he moved, with his considerable retinue and possessions, into a large town house which was to be paid for later.

One of the most important pictures of this period is *The Blinding of Samson* of 1636 (Frankfurt, Staedelsches Kunstinstitut). The 'thirties are frequently referred to as Rembrandt's Baroque phase when he adopted the Grand Manner—this is, in my opinion, only true in a limited sense. Admittedly, Samson was a favourite Baroque subject and Rembrandt's treatment of it has the rhythm and movement of a large Rubens composition, but how different it really is. Despite the gruesome portrayal of Samson's face as the soldier pushes a dagger deep into his eye, Rembrandt has made the foot convey all the victim's agony, juxtaposing it with the retreating figure of Delilah. The triumph of her expression is mixed with horror and apprehension at what she has done. (Saskia is, of course, the model here as in many of the portraits and narratives at this time.) The mythological picture of the same year, 1636, the *Danae* (Leningrad, Hermitage), shows him faultlessly portraying the rich fall of light on the soft flesh of Danae, one of Rembrandt's rare nudes, which are themselves among the few large-scale nudes in seventeenth-century Dutch Painting. The Danae typifies his approach at this period, where attention to detail is combined with smooth impasto, using deep rich colours and warm lighting. Naturally the underlying structure of the picture relies on the superb drawing of the figure.

It must not be forgotten, in discussing his rich variety of themes, that Rembrandt was an all-embracing artist in an age of specialists. The 'thirties produced still lifes and his first landscape paintings. Although he painted only about fifteen landscapes, he made many more drawings and etchings. These partly imaginary views have a broad atmospheric quality which greatly influenced Jacob Ruisdael, just as the monochrome range of tones impressed Van Goyen. Their majestic, mysterious spirit, partially derived from Hercules Seghers, could not be recaptured by other artists.

The next decade saw great changes in Rembrandt's fortunes. His mother, to whom he seems to have been deeply attached, died in 1640. This loss was compensated in the following year by the birth of a son, Titus, the only one of Saskia's four children to survive. Rembrandt's great affection for his son is clearly seen in his portraits of him. Perhaps the portrait of 1655 showing Titus writing at a desk (Rotterdam, Boymans Museum) is the most appealing.

In 1642 he completed the enormous *Night Watch*, and Saskia died. The importance of this year as a turning point in Rembrandt's career has been over-emphasised. Saskia had long been an invalid and her death could not have been an unexpected shock. Within three years he was happily living with the kindly Hendrickje Stoffels, who bore him a daughter in 1654. He could not marry Hendrickje without forfeiting Saskia's dowry. However much he may have been affected by the loss of those closest to him, his creative urge and his absorption in his work were by far the most important things to Rembrandt.

The Night Watch is the most written-about of all Rembrandt's works. The commission required him to work on an unfamilar scale—the canvas now measures 12 x 15 feet and was originally even larger. He rose to the challenge, creating a new formula for the large scale portrait of the Civic Guard, just as the *Anatomy Lesson* had been unprecedented in its field ten years earlier. In modern times removal of dirty varnishes revealed that it is a daylight scene, not a night watch, the shadows being caused by the surrounding buildings. Rembrandt has captured the commotion and noise of the assembling company—a musket has been fired in error—a group of children rush into their midst, with one running to the left—the lances and muskets emphasise the variety of directions and diagonals. Each face, even if it ought strictly to be in shadow, is caught by the same sunlight which falls with dazzling splendour on the two principal figures. It proved too personal and striking an innovation for the Company and the general public, and was not received with enthusiasm. The brilliant execution of such a compositional idea ranks among Rembrandt's greatest achievements, though it is not in my opinion his greatest work. During the 1640's Rembrandt became a thoroughly mature artist. At the same time, his desire to paint seems to have become stronger than ever. His technical mastery was becoming so complete that he could work more rapidly, leaving aside details for the essentials. The reflection of light from a figure or an object now begins almost to *represent* it, as for example in *The Adoration of the Shepherds* of 1646 (London, National Gallery). The movement and gesture of the previous decade were replaced by a more silent, undemonstrative, yet perfect communi-

cation between the minds of the figures. This is most touchingly shown in the *Holy Family with Angels* of 1645 (Leningrad, The Hermitage). Equally, in his portraits there is a deeper penetration into the thoughts of his subjects. The pattern for later development was set.

During the 1650's and 1660's he became totally absorbed in his inward creative urge and his paintings take on a highly personal, almost visionary, quality. The handling becomes increasingly broad and surfaces and outlines are broken up by the light. The eyes, in particular, dominate the face. Impasto becomes so thick that only a palette knife can put it on to the canvas and there mould it into shape—a technique of our own age. He was relatively unconcerned about his declining popularity and ultimate bankruptcy. The sale of his collection of pictures and drawings must, however, have been a bitter blow. Moreover, the gap between him and his contemporaries was being widened by the direction which Dutch life and art were beginning to take. The influence of French society in dress and manners brought a demand for small genre pictures of great delicacy and little significance. The pioneer spirit had given way to a settled existence of wealth and refinement. But to many important people, Rembrandt remained a pre-eminent figure. One of these, who was a close friend and patron, was Jan Six. His portrait of 1654, still in the possession of the Six family in Amsterdam, is undoubtedly one of Rembrandt's greatest portraits. In the previous year, his international reputation brought him a commission from a Sicilian nobleman. For this remote patron he painted in glowing, atmospheric tones the *Aristotle Contemplating the Bust of Homer*, recently bought by the Metropolitan Museum, New York. The same glowing red, green and gold of the Six portrait were used in the very moving scene, *Jacob Blessing the Sons of Joseph* 1656, (Kassel, Gemäldegalerie). In the self-portraits of this period he achieved his most serene and powerful effects. No spectator can remain unmoved beneath the gaze of the artist in the seated *Self-portrait* of 1658 (New York, Frick Collection).

Rembrandt's remaining years, until his death in 1669, saw him produce many masterful pictures, intensely moving expressions of a philosophy enriched by experience and saddened by age. His range of technique and compositional invention are shown in two works of

Plate 1. HENDRICK TERBRUGGEN (Deventer 1588 - Utrecht 1629):
Jacob, Laban and Leah. Oil on canvas, 98 x 115 cm (38³/₄ x 45 ins). London, National Gallery.

1662: *The Syndics of the Drapers Guild* (Amsterdam, Rijksmuseum) and *The Conspiracy of Julius Civilis* (Stockholm, National Museum). Both were important commissions. In the first, the attention of the group at the meeting centres on a figure in their audience who has, perhaps, asked a question. There is wonderful variety in the momentary reactions of each figure to this disturbance, recalling the captured gesture of Jan Six pulling on his gloves. The huge candle-lit scene, *The Conspiracy of Julius Civilis,* represents the artist's most extreme use of light and his greatest freedom of method. Perhaps the most emotional work of his late years is *The Return of the Prodigal Son* (Leningrad, The Hermitage). Utterly simple in design and without movement, veiled in a vibrating light, it succeeds in laying bare with great compassion the frailty and complexity of the human soul. However great our admiration for Rembrandt, there can be no doubt that he himself was never satisfied with what he had done and did not find a solution to the many problems which he saw in human existence. His doubts and disillusionment speak loudly in the searching self-analysis of the later self-portraits. In studying Rembrandt, we are continually confronted with that inexplicable quality which belongs only to the universal genius.

Although Rembrandt's influence was so far-reaching in Dutch art, only one of his actual pupils, Carel Fabritius, seems to have grasped something of his spirit. His career ended tragically at the age of 32, when he was killed in the Delft explosion in 1654. From the few of his works that survive, the influence of Rembrandt is clear, particularly in his *Self-portrait* (Rotterdam, Boymans Museum), but, unlike Rembrandt, he used a very light background in most of his pictures. Fabritius, who was probably the master of Vermeer at Delft, forms an important link between his own master and his own pupil.

In 1632, as Amsterdam marvelled at the unveiling of Rembrandt's *Anatomy Lesson,* Delft was the scene of the unheralded birth of another truly great artist, Jan Vermeer. The immediate contrast between the paintings of Rembrandt and Vermeer, working within a short distance of each other in the 1660's, presents an interesting problem. Even though Fabritius may have helped to bridge the gap between them, this hardly offers a full explanation. While Rembrandt takes warm browns and greys to probe the depths of shadow and half-light, Vermeer delights in strong sunlight, using pure white, light yellows and blues. Yet, whatever the difference in their approach, both artists share a fascination for the properties of light. A similarity also appears in the spirit of their pictures. Vermeer must surely have learned from Rembrandt's early works, where small figures, often called 'Philosophers,' seem isolated and introspective, almost dwarfed by their surroundings. So many of Vermeer's young females seem entirely absorbed in their thoughts and occupations, as is *The Lady with a Lute* (New York, Metropolitan Museum), who gazes out of the window. Equally, could Vermeer have failed to grasp the poetic calm in Rembrandt's portraits of young girls? How close is the spiritual relationship between Rembrandt's *Girl at a Window Sill* (London, Dulwich College Gallery) and Vermeer's *Girl with a Flute* (Washington, National Gallery), painted about twenty years later.

This indefinable spiritual quality helps to lift Vermeer far above his contemporaries, the painters of fashionable genre. The other outstanding and distinguishing features are his approach to daylight and his technique of painting what it revealed to him. Here lies the mystery of his genius, from which flowed creations of an entirely new and unprecedented kind.

The origins of his style are, as it were, complicated by the presence of two early works, now generally accepted, which show the distinct influence of Italy through the Utrecht School. The *Diana and her Companions* (The Hague, Mauritshuis) of 1655 seems an isolated work unrelated to his normal type of intimate interior scene, and quite different in treatment. Perhaps, although the feeling is Italianate, the actual choice of subject and the composition were influenced by Rembrandt's *Bathsheba at her Toilet* (Paris, Louvre), painted in the previous year. The majority of his works depict an elaborate interior with one or two figures, engaged in everyday activities, the lady of the house reading or writing letters, entertaining a guest or playing a musical instrument, while servants are shown about their work in the kitchen. Most of the ladies' activities were the common subject matter of the so-called society or fashionable genre painters, but one of Vermeer's most popular pictures is an exception showing a servant as the only figure in the painting, the *Maidservant pouring Milk* (Amsterdam, Rijksmuseum). It has the feeling of a portrait of a well-known family servant, and can hardly have been intended for sale.

This point brings up the importance of the background to Vermeer's work as an artist. In speaking of Vermeer, no mention has so far been made of the most astonishing aspects of his achievement. One might have been discussing the career of a normal artist, but nothing could be further from reality. Although very little mention is made of him in contemporary sources, it is clear that he was not a professional artist, in the sense of earning his living from painting. Although qualified as a master, he earned his living as an art dealer and tavern keeper, businesses which he had inherited from his father. The leisure allowed to him from these occupations must have been quite small, as he had an ever increasing family to support; he was in fact survived by eight children under age and three married ones. Despite his premature death at the age of 43, he had a working life as a master of over twenty years. Yet there are today less than forty paintings in existence by Vermeer. Even allowing for losses, this is surely the output of a spare-time artist. Vermeer must have treated his painting, his personal study of the magic of sunlight, almost as a hobby to be taken up whenever business permitted. When his work is considered in this way, the more incredibile are the results he achieved. His paintings have a plein-air effect, a startling freshness that seems to belong to the Impressionist era rather than the seventeenth century. Even his ' pointillist ' use of dots of colour to catch the light seems to belong to that later age. He combined a baffling perfection of technique with a delicate sense of pure colour, magically seen in the real light of day. Absorbed in exterior reality, Vermeer brings no unhappiness, no drama, into his highly personal art. He might be called the greatest ' still-life ' painter of human life.

By some strange twist of history, Vermeer became a totally forgotten artist until his ' re-discovery ' in the late nineteenth century. Until this re-discovery, and for a time afterwards, his pictures were attributed to another artist who worked in Delft at the same period, Pieter de Hoogh. In 1653, de Hoogh came from Rotterdam to Delft, where he married and settled happily for a decade. During these ten years he produced his greatest pictures. The domestic scenes, especially those in the open air, are close in lighting and colour to Vermeer, but despite this similarity he cannot be truly called a rival to Vermeer. De Hoogh's work represents the greatest domestic genre painting of the Dutch School, but Vermeer's art rises above genre painting to a category where there are no competitors. For the last twenty years of his career, de Hoogh became a painter of upper class society in The Hague and Amsterdam. His later work consists mainly of interior scenes, which are much more subdued than anything he painted in Delft and they are not today considered to be of the same importance.

If interior scenes were the favourite subject of so many famous artists, there was no lack of talent to portray the exteriors of buildings and the appearance of the streets and squares. Vermeer painted two views of this kind, the view from his window looking across the street, called *The Little Street in Delft* (Amsterdam, Rijksmuseum) and the famous *View of Delft* (The Hague, Mauritshuis). These are the finest townscapes of the Dutch School. Indeed, the *View of Delft* has few parallels in the history of painting, although Vermeer was not, of course, a specialist. The best specialist townscape painters were Jan van der Heyden, and the brothers Job (1630-1693) and Gerrit Berckheyde (1638-1698) from Haarlem. Of these, Van der Heyden produced the most highly finished scenes, the composition and atmospheric lighting of which are, in general, more varied and interesting. The exacting standards of draughtsmanship, perspective and detail closely resemble the work of the great specialist of the church interior, Pieter Saenredam, who also painted exterior scenes.

The same degree of attention to detail and surface texture typifies many of the best genre painters of the second half of the century. The history of Holland is the most eloquently illustrated story of activity and animation. The genre picture, covering the life of the Dutch at every level, held the widest appeal, surpassing even the landscape in popularity. In the second half of the century, the nation was enjoying the wealth and security achieved in the period of expansion and endeavour. The barrack-room scenes of Dirck Hals (1591-1656) and Willem Duyster (1599-1635) were forgotten in the enthusiasm for the elegant example of France in the art of gracious living. The later works of de Hoogh show the scale and magnificence of the rooms, with richly dressed ladies engaged in suitably delicate

Plate 2. FRANS HALS (Antwerp 1580/5 - Haarlem 1666):
A Family Group in a Landscape. Oil on canvas, 149 x 252 cm (58$\frac{1}{2}$ x 98$\frac{3}{4}$ ins). London, National Gallery.

Plate 3. REMBRANDT VAN RIJN (Leyden 1606 - Amsterdam 1669):
The Woman Taken in Adultery. Oil on panel, 81 x 64 cm (33 x 25$\frac{3}{4}$ ins). London, National Gallery.

occupations, especially the playing of various instruments. The taste for musical parties is mirrored in the many intimate and charming works of the great masters of this art, Gabriel Metsu (1629-1667) and Gerard Terborch (1617-1681). They tell their stories and record the events of the household with the greatest delicacy of brushwork, giving many of their small pictures the quality of sparkling gems. Metsu and the lesser figure of Frans van Mieris (1635-1681) were pupils of Gerard Dou (1613-1675) who had studied under Rembrandt and become one of the first painters of middle class life. The other Rembrandt pupil who excelled in these scenes was Nicholaes Maes (1632-1693) an artist most deeply and happily influenced by the poetic and thoughtful charm of his teacher.

Scenes from the less refined atmosphere of the tavern found an equally enthusiastic market. The most prolific painter of peasant life was Adriaen van Ostade (1610-1684). His finest work recalls the benefit he received from his association with the great Adrian Brouwer, mingled with the influence of Rembrandt chiaroscuro. These artists who sought to capture the momentary attitudes and actions of the crowded tavern relied on the speed and facility of their draughts-manship, although Ostade's later work on a larger scale tends to be more colourful and highly finished. A special place in genre paintings is held by Jan Steen, a remarkable figure who was not only a highly gifted and inventive artist but a humorous and independent spirit in a somewhat sedate age. He successfully painted a wide range of subjects, but the most popular works are undoubtedly his small intimate genre scenes and the large-scale tavern and family groups. In his marriage to Jan van Goyen's daughter he found an ideally gay partner who delighted to act as his model. Steen also enjoyed depicting himself in the midst of his own family and friends, as in the famous *Merry Company* (The Hague, Mauritshuis). Despite a certain unevenness in the quality of his work, Steen is outstanding for his variety, compositional invention, and the way he delightfully imbued his paintings with the spirit of his own personality.

As Evelyn wrote in 1641, landscapes enjoyed a popularity rivalling the appeal of the many forms of genre painting. To English collectors in particular, they became the most admired achievements of the Dutch School. In the seventeenth century, the Dutch had a deep-rooted interest in landscape painting. It went beyond the natural desire to portray the countryside that they had fought so hard to possess. Had this not been so, it would be hard to explain their interest in sunlit Italian views and Alpine panoramas, though native views of Holland were the most popular subjects. To many visitors, Holland's landscape is monotonously flat, but to the Dutch artist it was a fascinating subject because the huge, cloudy skies are constantly changing and so changed the lighting and atmosphere of the landscape—all Dutch painting is characterised by an interest in light and atmosphere. As in all other types of painting, great artists appeared whose development of landscape painting towards modern form is to many people the outstanding achievement of the Golden Age of Dutch art. The seventeenth century saw the emergence of landscape painting as a major art to which, together with Claude Lorrain, Holland made the greatest contribution.

The first decade of the century was a period of transition from the older Flemish ideal of landscape to a more naturalistic Dutch style. Gillis van Coninxloo (1544-1607), a Flemish born artist who settled in Amsterdam, was the key figure, providing a link between the two schools.

Coninxloo generally retained the traditional and often unrealistic Flemish division in depth, dark blue background, green middle ground and warm foreground, but gave a degree of realistic lighting and detail to his work. The combination in Coninxloo of fantasy and naturalism appealed to his two important pupils Hercules Seghers and Esias van de Velde, who joined the Haarlem Guild together in 1612.

But for the existence of Hercules Seghers, Rembrandt would be the only Dutch artist whose work has an almost frightening power and mystery inherent in it. Rembrandt's unreserved admiration for Seghers' work makes this comparison valid, for no other contemporary artist took such heed of Seghers. Like Rembrandt, Seghers was a great artist who seems to have pursued an illusive personal vision throughout his life.

Seghers was primarily an etcher and, although he may have painted over a hundred paintings, there are only about fifteen accepted pictures known today. This loss added to the lack of documentary knowledge has made the study of Seghers and particularly the chronology of his work very difficult. Born at

Haarlem in 1589 or 1590, he clearly began his studies at an early age. In 1606, his teacher Coninxloo died, and at the sale of his possessions Seghers bought the majority of the paintings and prints which he had probably studied as a pupil. These included works by sixteenth-century German artists such as Altdorfer (Coninxloo had worked in Frankenthal), Pieter Bruegel and various contemporary artists. These influences can be traced in Seghers' style; of his contemporaries or immediate forerunners, the mountain landscapes of De Momper and Savery seem to have impressed him.

During the next few years, Seghers almost certainly made a journey to the Alps. The vastness and desolate grandeur of Alpine panoramas made a lasting impression on the young artist. Though he had seen the scenes depicted by other artists, his personal experience of the mountains fired his imagination. To this subject he devoted most of his etchings and paintings, and the remainder are rarely without some reference to that strange wilderness, part real, part imagined, which mountain scenery represented to Seghers. The importance of these mountain views is that, however unreal the subject, Seghers could apply accuracy to the details, to the fall of light, to the mood, in a way that was in advance of others, succeeding in giving a strong feeling of reality to the subject. The massed groups of jagged rocks, the sheer walls rising from valleys, the stark trees, all help to point to the elemental, timeless forces of nature as the subject of wonderment and awe, an ominous effect heightened by the absence of figures in most of his work. Throughout his career he made many experiments with his etchings, exploring the possibilities of the medium. Seghers' powers as a draughtsman enabled him to suggest a great deal with a very few strokes.

In pursuing his personal vision he eventually suffered poverty and despair, leading to his early death in the 1630's. The monumental mountain panoramas evoke a tragic mood which obviously influenced Rembrandt profoundly, as he owned eight Seghers paintings. On the infrequent occasions when Seghers turned his attention to a realistic landscape of the Dutch countryside, the results were immediately a step forward in the development of landscape painting. In his two *Views of Rhenen* (Berlin, Dahlem Museum), the low viewpoint, the accurate monochrome

tonal values, the structure beneath the fluid technique, impressed not only Rembrandt and Philips Koninck (1619-1688) but also Van Goyen. The latter may have found the approach and technique instructive, but he was not attracted by the mood. In an age of optimism, Seghers struck a note of spiritual drama which was only understood by Rembrandt and Jacob Ruisdael.

Coninxloo's other pupil, Esias van de Velde (1591-1630) followed up the realistic aspects of his master's style and applied them in an atmospheric way to purely Dutch scenes. He still selected and ordered his compositions in a slightly formalised way, as for example in *The Ferry* of 1622 (Amsterdam, Rijksmuseum). Jan van Goyen began painting in exactly this style with the same colourful palette but, as already mentioned, he soon developed a harmonious, monochrome style of a much more modern kind. From the 1640's onwards, he was able to paint with superbly fluent strokes. Van Goyen was the most prolific Dutch landscape artist, producing several thousand paintings and drawings in his lifetime. His treatment of skies was outstandingly skilful and so modern that his pictures hang happily with those of Jongkind and Boudin.

Salomon van Ruysdael (about 1600-1670) was Van Goyen's rival in output and popularity. Their early work was very similar, in fact, in composition and colouring. A typical scene is a river with fishermen in a boat, dominated by a graceful tree against a bright sky. Ruysdael continued to paint these simple, well balanced compositions in broad strokes with gleaming blue water, rich green foliage, and a creamy sky. He was not the rival of Van Goyen in variety of composition or atmosphere, but together they met the huge demand for unambitious, harmonious landscapes whose great beauty derived from their simple truth to nature.

However large the output of Van Goyen and Salomon van Ruysdael, it represents, of course, only one aspect of the development of landscape painting. To many modern critics, the achievements of these two were surpassed by Dordrecht's famous painter Aelbert Cuyp (1620-1691). Cuyp began painting estuary scenes in the manner of Van Goyen and Ruysdael, but soon developed his own style and became a very versatile artist. The decisive factor for Cuyp was the influence of the Dutch Italianate or ' Romanist '

Plate 5. REMBRANDT VAN RIJN:
The Denial of St Peter (detail). Oil on canvas. Amsterdam, Rijksmuseum.

Plate 4. REMBRANDT VAN RIJN:
Portrait of Baartjen Maartens, wife of Herman Doomer (detail). Oil on canvas. Leningrad, Hermitage.

painters. Though he never went to Italy himself, he gained from them a lifelong interest in warm sunlight, which he applied not to Italianate subjects but to scenes in Holland, enveloping rivers, cattle and buildings, in the hazy golden tones of sunlight. The combination of warm sunlight and Dutch scenery makes his work distinctive and appealing. Cuyp exerted a strong influence on the eighteenth-century landscape painters of England, where so many of his pictures are today. Of these, the finest is the unsurpassed *View of Dordrecht* (Kenwood, Iveagh Bequest). He painted this view of his native city seen across the broad expanse of the Maas river shimmering in that golden light on which Cuyp's fame so securely rests. Cuyp's talent for painting cattle in a landscape was only surpassed by Paulus Potter (1625-54). Potter started painting at a precociously early age and was able to produce a considerable number of pictures before his death at the age of twenty-nine. His work is remarkable for the meticulous technique which brings out every detail of the subject with painstaking fidelity to nature. His cattle seem somehow larger than life, evoking a naive sense of nature's power of creation, where man's existence is unimportant. His powers of artistry and evocation are best seen in his famous picture *The Bull* (The Hague, Mauritshuis).

It would be reasonable to suppose that the work of even the most enthusiastic landscape painter would stop at nightfall, but so intense and varied was the interest of the Dutch that even the moonlight called forth its own great artist, Aert van der Neer (1603-1677). He was fascinated by the night sky and the fall of moonlight on a landscape. The full extent of his skill in this self-chosen art is best seen in the winter views, where the moonlight falls on snow-covered trees and frozen rivers and small dark figures are silhouetted against the whiteness of the snow and moonlight. Though regarded as a popular amateur artist in his lifetime, Van der Neer combines an astonishingly modern concept of the night scene with a romantic spirit that will always ensure his place as an important individualist in the richness of Dutch landscape painting.

Like many artistic developments, the Dutch landscape came to a summit of achievement worthy of the whole movement. The artist who represents the high point of the Dutch genius for landscape is, of course, Jacob van Ruisdael, who could reasonably be claimed as one of the very greatest exponents of the art the world has ever seen. Ruisdael is the ideal culmination for a variety of reasons, all of which are typically Dutch and characteristic of what we know of the school. He had a deep love for nature, a complete grasp of the light and atmosphere of a landscape, and a feeling for detail and exactness which was never allowed to exclude that sensitivity to the poetic and the romantic which is the true meeting of art and representation. He was, like Rembrandt, passionately and exclusively devoted to his work, and a deeply religious man, a member of the Mennonites, with whom Rembrandt was also closely associated. Both Rembrandt and Ruisdael had a natural inclination to a spiritual and emotional unrest which ruled the underlying mood of their work. Ruisdael, who never married, seems to have sought the company of the field and forest rather than that of his fellow beings. His emotional troubles were accompanied by physical suffering from a chronic disease in the last fifteen years of his life. The particular characteristics of his work which are immediately recognisable are his understanding of trees, with their power of expressing a mood, and his awareness of the effect of wind blowing across a landscape or forest, majestically stirring trees and moving clouds.

Ruisdael, received as a master in 1648, began his career in the then established manner of Vroom and of his uncle, Salomon van Ruysdael. A journey through the German forests two years later seems to have greatly inspired him. His outlook expanded through contact with the Utrecht School and the large panoramic views of Philips Koninck whose palette also attracted him. At the same time, he was a sufficiently great artist to understand the monumental aspects of landscapes by Seghers and Rembrandt. After this formative period in the 'fifties, he settled in Amsterdam in 1656.

The fascination of the forest and woodland clearing provided the subjects of many of his works, and his palette was dominated by a variety of greens. The grandeur of his large pictures does not always hold the same appeal as the rarer views of purely Dutch scenes, painted on a much smaller scale. A view of Haarlem across a calm vista of superbly painted fields and hedges, where shadows of clouds break up the reflections of daylight, would be a typical example of the small landscapes. His coast scenes and winter landscapes, painted in a similar spirit, add to our understanding of his versatility. The essential quality which Ruisdael possessed, and which is in everything he painted, was his sense of structure. His landscapes have a more complex and more clearly conveyed structure than those of any other Dutch artist. Others had the fluidity, the knowledge of light, the colours, but Ruisdael embraced all these and added to them what was often lacking—a convincing structure. The famous *Windmill at Wijk* (Amsterdam, Rijksmuseum) of 1670, one of his greatest creations, is a perfect example of this build-up of a picture's structure, very much a concealed aspect of painting. The *Windmill* also shows, in the scale of the three figures, that Ruisdael, like many Dutch artists, felt the infinite, timeless grandeur of nature where human beings are dwarfed into insignificance. During his last years, he was attracted to the forest scenes of Everdingen, who had visited Sweden and introduced rugged forest scenes with mountain torrents. Ruisdael interpreted these in a mood of mystery and tragedy, but without, in many cases, the power and skill of his earlier works. These late forest views appear like a 'modern' recapturing of the old fascination which woodlands had always held for the earliest northern landscape painters. A tribute to Ruisdael, giving an indication of his later influence, came from Constable, who wrote in a letter to Leslie, " I have seen an affecting picture this morning by Ruisdael, it haunts my mind and clings to my heart, and stands between you and me while I am talking to you ".

Meindert Hobbema was Ruisdael's only important pupil, but his work obviously appears limited by comparison. Hobbema worked in a very different spirit, a spirit of calm, balanced harmony where the mood is one of optimism. He became very repetitious as he arranged his stock of motifs in a limited variety of compositions, but his pictures are usually very delicately and skilfully painted in an attractive range of colours.

In *The Avenue at Middelharnis* (London, National Gallery), Hobbema found a unique moment in his career. Few paintings have been more widely known and reproduced.

Such was the wealth of ability and inspiration in marine painting and still life, that one cannot, within the scope of a brief survey, adequately include those masters who brought their art to the same perfections as were achieved in landscape painting. Their achievements are here well represented in famous pictures by Jan van de Cappelle and the two princes of still-life paintings: Willem Kalf and Jan Davidsz. de Heem.

By the time of Jacob Ruisdael's death in 1682, the era in the art of a nation, which we can only attempt to describe by calling it ' The Golden Age,' was rapidly coming to an end. The resources of the Dutch people were strained by the conflict with the rising power of Louis XIV. The artistic leadership began to change hands and the Dutch patrons no longer found satisfaction in the creations of their own countrymen. Dutch artists of the eighteenth century found themselves without creative genius and dumbly carried on the style of their great predecessors, completely left behind by the taste of a new age. The stage which had witnessed such an amazing performance was deserted.

THE PLATES

Plate 1—HENDRICK TERBRUGGEN: Jacob, Laban and Leah. Hendrick Terbrugghen belongs to that group of great Dutch artists who inexplicably remained unknown or unacclaimed until our own century. The ' discovery' of Terbrugghen has brought an understanding of his peculiar qualities and his importance to the Utrecht School, which carried the art of the Mediterranean to Dutch painting.

Terbrugghen, born in 1588, was of a well-established Catholic family living near Deventer. As a child, he was taken to Utrecht where he began studying at a very early age in the studio of Abraham Bloemaert (1564-1651). This apprenticeship must have been brief because Terbrugghen left for Italy when he was not more than 15 or 16 years old. What prompted him to make the long journey at this age we can only guess. He stayed in Italy, living mainly in Rome, for ten years before returning to Utrecht in 1614. In 1617 he was admitted to the Guild of Utrecht, but it is not known whether he remained in Utrecht without interruption until his death there in 1629, aged 42. Terbrugghen seems to have been a retiring and unnoticed personality, unlike his contemporary Honthorst, who gained a considerable reputation in Holland and Italy. There is no record of Terbrugghen

Plate 6. HERCULES SEGHERS (Haarlem 1589/90 - The Hague 1638):
Landscape or Great Mountain View. Oil on canvas, 37.5 x 100 cm (14⅞ x 39¼ ins). Florence, Uffizi.

Plate 7. PIETER SAENREDAM (Assendelft 1597 - Haarlem 1665):
St James, Utrecht. Oil on panel, 56 x 48 cm (22¼ x 18¼ ins). Munich, Alte Pinakothek.

having received any commissions in Italy, and there are no certain works painted before he was thirty. Caravaggio was at the height of his fame (or notoriety) when Terbrugghen came to Rome, and it is clear that he made a great impact on the Northern artist.

Terbrugghen also studied the artists who followed Caravaggio's lead both in Rome and Naples. If paintings by Terbrugghen during his Italian stay are found, they will probably be far more pronouncedly Caravaggesque in every way than his earliest known work, which dates from well after his return to Utrecht. His early contacts in Bloemaert's studio with the work of sixteenth-century Netherlandish and German artists were submerged by the effect of Caravaggio, but were not forgotten. When he returned to Utrecht, the memories of these early compositions were revived, and his earliest works are as much indebted to Dürer as to Caravaggio. Such is the case with his earliest dated work *The Crowning with Thorns* (Copenhagen, State Museum) and *The Beheading of St John* (Edinburgh, National Gallery of Scotland) which belongs to the same period. Terbrugghen treats the ' closed ' frontal compositions of Dürer with the colouring and superb chiaroscuro of Caravaggio. The archaic feeling in much of his early work is also conveyed by the use of sixteenth-century types. Memories of Massys are forcefully conjured up by the old men with spectacles crouched over tables.

Terbrugghen rapidly improved the quality of his draughtsmanship and his application of the brushstroke, so that his pictures seem suddenly to become more beautiful. The lighting ceased to be over-emphatic, becoming delicate and subtle, but losing nothing of its importance in his work. Genre pictures, on Caravaggesque themes—for example *The Flute-players* (Cassel, Museum) were interspersed with the numerous Biblical subjects which were the major achievements of his brief decade of known activity. Terbrugghen's religious works are characterised by a calm intensity, a compassion, and a sense of sincerity and devotion, which is never without restraint and humility. The genre pictures sometimes show a bravura of technique which is unlike his usual free but deliberate application of paint. Terbrugghen's immense sensitivity to light and surface texture is best seen in the turbanned head of the boy in the *Vocation of St Matthew* (Utrecht, Central Museum) of 1621. This is a frequently reproduced detail,

yet no clearer illustration could be given of Terbrugghen's message to Vermeer. He was the first Dutch artist to bring to Holland the full impact of Caravaggio, and it is a measure of Terbrugghen's ability that he was more than equal to the task.

The *Jacob and Laban* (London, National Gallery) is signed and dated 1627. Its full title tells the story of the scene: Jacob reproaching Laban for giving him Leah in place of Rachel. Jacob has been cruelly deceived by his uncle, Laban, who had substituted his elder daughter, Leah, for Rachel on the wedding night. Jacob, after toiling seven years to gain the hand of his beloved Rachel, now bursts out angrily at the deceivers, while Rachel watches almost unnoticed in the background. The emotions are wonderfully conveyed by the expressions and gestures. Jacob points vigorously in accusation, but Laban raises his hand hesitantly to restrain Jacob and at the same time to make his point that Leah was the first-born. We can sense how Jacob's anger is only just breaking through his astonishment. Leah is trying to remain calm and disdainful, but Laban's face betrays his discomfort and concern at what is happening. Terbrugghen fills the scene with emotion and gesture, yet even these are contained by the overall calm, static feeling which dominates most of his work. The two figures on each side balance each other across the middle of the picture where Terbrugghen has made the finished meal of the story into one of his finest still lives. Glass, metal, bread and cloth are all transformed by the fall of light, and given an uncanny naturalism. A complete, masterly still-life composition exists like a painting within a painting. It is the light that gives these objects their naturalism, and to paint them like this called for an ' impressionist ' type of brushstroke, quite different from the minute rendering of most contemporary Dutch still-life painters. No other chandelier was painted in this way in 1627.

One of the most striking features of the *Jacob and Laban* is the unusually powerful colours in the garments, the bright red singling out the central figure and contrasting with the coolness of the bluish grey table cloth. It is the half tones of reflections and shadows which reveal his typical subtlety of colour. His composition has the strong diagonal accent used in many of these scenes. The same subject was treated yet again by Terbrugghen in a slighter and later work at

Cologne, where, in a less compact composition, he achieved the same compelling effects.

Plate 2—FRANS HALS: A Family Group in a Landscape.

Frans Hals was the first great artist of the Dutch School. The most remarkable feature of the development of the Dutch School in the seventeenth century was how its three truly great artists rose one after another to mark the stages of development, each stage dominated by the character of their individual genius. The story rests on the achievements of the three giants, Hals, Rembrandt and Vermeer.

As in the case of Terbrugghen, there is no record of the early style of Hals before his first documented picture, painted at the age of at least thirty, in 1616. Having arrived in Haarlem from Antwerp in 1591, he may have been apprenticed soon afterwards to Carel van Mander. The early records indicate that Hals was a boisterous character who drank a good deal, got into debt, was sued by his creditors, and even had troubles with the painters' Guild. His first wife died in 1615 and he was left with two small children. The sale of his house followed her death. Two years later he married a loyal companion who stayed with him throughout his career, very much for richer or poorer, and they had at least ten children, making it increasingly difficult to earn sufficient money. Debt and misfortune were his lifelong companions, but the sorrowful conditions of his last years were unusually pitiful even in the histories of great artists. Yet, whatever the circumstances of his life, Hals, like Rembrandt, not only kept his powers as a creative artist, but increased them. Much has been made of his Flemish origins to explain his exuberant recklessness. No explanation or apology is needed; without vitality and spirit in the man, there could be none in his work. The most important experiences he gained from contacts with Antwerp were firstly a knowledge of Rubens' sense of colour and approach, and secondly, a similar understanding, through Bloemaert, of the sixteenth-century Venetian artists. These influences help to explain how, in the first group of 1616, the Banquet of the Officers of St George (Haarlem, Frans Hals Museum) he could work so freely on a large scale, and make such superb use of the brightest colour.

What an impact this group must have made in Haarlem, and far beyond! It was a new concept of group portraiture not only in composition but colour, and, above all, in the animation of faces and gestures. Hals captured the jovial, festive mood of the occasion —the military groups were no longer the serious austere men who had fought for the independence of the nation. He removed self-consciousness from the sitters, creating not only a true portrait, but a complete picture in its own right.

Though he introduced a new compositional spirit, a new feeling for colour, yet the true basis of his success, and indeed his greatness as a painter, lay in his ability to handle the brush. Far from being an over-simplification of the style of the artist, this is the essence of Hals. He was possessed of a faultless, first-time touch which laid the paint on in precisely the right way on precisely the right spot. It enabled him to put down on the canvas his immediate, emotional reaction to the subject in front of him, before the inspiration could pass. This quality was shared in the seventeenth century by Velazquez alone, and remained an isolated phenomenon until the career of Edouard Manet. Proof of this fact is simple. Hals' qualities of handling are seen at their height in his second portrait of the Officers of St George, painted in 1627. If we try to compare their treatment to contemporary portraits or landscapes, the tightly painted, detailed portraits of Miereveld or the earliest landscapes of Van Goyen, it is clear that comparison is impossible: Hals was in a different and completely 'modern' category. He drew and painted the subject throughout with the same rapid sweeps and flicks of the brush that somehow bring through to us, undiminished, the power and immediacy of his creative energy. This distinctive brushwork is obvious even in his earliest single portraits where he did rely on tradition and precedent, and where he gave great attention to detail. Yet even in the detail of a lace collar he was able to paint more freely and forcefully than such contemporaries as Miereveld and Ravesteyn. The Laughing Cavalier of 1624 (London, Wallace Collection) shows exactly his treatment of such details. Equally distinctive from an early date is the self-assurance of his sitters, seen in their posture as much as in their facial expression. It is understandable that this was a reflection of the artist's personality (and he had every justification for being sure of himself). His tech-

Plate 8. GABRIEL METSU (Leyden 1629 - Amsterdam 1667):
A Woman seated at a Table and a Man tuning a Violin. Oil on panel, 41 x 36 cm (17 x 14³/₄ ins). London, National Gallery.

Plate 9. PIETER DE HOOGH (Rotterdam 1629 - Amsterdam c. 1684):
The Courtyard of a House in Delft. Oil on panel, 73 x 62 cm (29 x 23 ¹/₂ ins). London, National Gallery.

nique broadened considerably in his middle period, where he found his greatest freedom in gay, informal portraits of peasant girls and young boys in fur hats. Most of his portraits share the same happy confident expression, seemingly rejoiceful at simply being alive.

Hals is inevitably compared to Rembrandt, and found to be a superficial and casual artist by comparison. This cannot be denied, but it is a revelation to see the results of the influence of the mature Rembrandt on Hals. In 1664, he painted the group of the *Governesses of the Almshouse* (Haarlem, Frans Hals Museum). Here, at the very end of his life, Hals achieved a penetration and sincerity in the faces of his sitters, and created an atmosphere around them, worthy of Rembrandt himself, but painted with the inimitable broadness of Hals. This rather severe group of elderly females, all in simple black and white, is the complete answer to those who would accuse him of being a purely superficial portrait painter. Fortunately for posterity, they, together with most of his finest groups, are still in the almshouse in Haarlem, which has become the best memorial to Frans Hals.

The *Family Group in a Landscape* dates from the late 1640's, when Hals had lost nothing of his vitality but blended it with greater sensitivity to mood and sentiment. Few artists could paint a family group of ten figures on such a large scale without losing their harmony and intimacy. Each figure has been placed, not only for the sake of composition, but to indicate their position in the family. Like all of Hals' work, the group portrait has that presence and vitality that never fails to strike the spectator. The figures are in excellent condition, allowing us to see the full beauty of his brushwork. The choice of colour and the subtlety of lighting again prove that only an artist of Rembrandt's stature could influence Hals. In this portrait Hals shows himself, like Rembrandt, to be a warm, human artist who must, again like Rembrandt, remain in a category of his own.

Plate 3—REMBRANDT VAN RIJN: The Woman Taken in Adultery. The National Gallery holds few paintings as profound and beautiful as Rembrandt's *The Woman Taken in Adultery*. It was painted in 1644 at that period of adversity in his life when he turned more passionately than ever before to the

stories of Christ's life on earth. To the middle 'forties belong the most intimate and simple conceptions of the *Holy Famyly*, and the *Adoration of the Magi*. Rembrandt had achieved a perfect balance in the portrayal of the divine in the terms of ordinary human life. The new warmth of colour and chiaroscuro which he had found in the *Night Watch*, he now used in these small-scale religious pictures. They have a sense of religious faith that can only be compared, whatever the formal differences, to the devotional pictures of earlier centuries, painted for private chapels and individual worship.

In *The Woman Taken in Adultery*, Rembrandt turned back to a type of composition used in his very early pictures, for example the *Simon in the Temple* (The Hague, Mauritshuis) of 1631. Both compositions show figures in a strong light, set back from the foreground and surrounded by the dark vastness of the imagined Temple. Yet whatever the similarities of composition, there is a complete contrast in the colouring and tone of the two pictures. In the later picture, the cool tones, with greyish white light detaching the group from the blackness of the background, are replaced by warmth of light and colour. Rembrandt succeeds in leaving the figures in their setting and at the same time brings them forward from the background. This background is sumptuously painted in rich browns with the warm light falling on the golden altar with reds and greens that echo the colours in the main group. There is a brilliant contrast between the white of the accused and the dark robes of the Pharisees who have interrupted Christ's teaching in the Temple, to bring their accusations to tempt Him. It is the most dramatic moment of the story when they wait to see if He will give judgement against the adulteress.

Though the painting of the background would tend to date the picture, the figures are painted with an attention to detail and finish, which is unlike the rapid handling of the nearly contemporary *Adoration* scenes, where details dissolve in the light. The explanation is that this was an especially important commission, possibly painted for Jan Six himself, which required such care and attention. It was noted in 1657, when in the possession of an Amsterdam dealer, as the most valuable picture in his inventory.

The Woman Taken in Adultery can be discussed and admired, but the way in which it was painted cannot be explained. The light which falls so strongly on the principal figures is at once natural and yet unreal. It seems to have an existence of its own, full of mystery and a sense of the divine, as it spreads into the recesses of the magnificent image of the Holy Temple. These effects of a magical light were not limited to paintings, for we find the same beauty in the famous *Hundred Gilder Print* created at the same period. The way that Rembrandt can create such a light and use it to such effect has neither explanation nor parallel in the history of painting. St John's account of the woman taken in adultery tells how, after Christ had told the woman to go and sin no more, He turned to them and said, " I am the light of the world: he that followeth me shall not walk in darkness, but shall have the light of life."

Plate 4—REMBRANDT VAN RIJN: Portrait of Baartjen Maartens, wife of Herman Doomer (*detail*). So thoroughly did Rembrandt explore the range of Biblical subjects, that it is easy to forget that two-thirds of his output of paintings were portraits. It would be wrong to think that this high proportion of portraits was governed by the need to earn a living. Though this may have been true in the earlier years, a survey of the whole of his portrait painting shows that over half of them were painted only because Rembrandt chose to do so.

In the early 1630's, after his arrival in Amsterdam and the success of *The Anatomy Lesson*, he faced strong competition for portrait commissions. Patrons wanted realism, accuracy and dignity in their portraits, and to win favour over his rivals, Rembrandt had to achieve a more complete illusion of reality. Rembrandt realised that others had given the maximum possible attention to the details of the face and garments, and that it would be impossible to improve on this aspect of their portraits. He certainly equalled them in this respect, but surpassed them by his ability to give a more realistic and atmospheric lighting to a portrait. In a strange fashion he suggested a space around the sitter, but, at the same time, seemed to let the figure project itself forward from the canvas. His superior understanding of light allowed him to give the figure more plasticity, although the outlines seem less sharp than in the work of his contemporaries. It also enabled him to make the modelling of the face more convincing. By varying the type of atmosphere he created around a figure, Rembrandt could enhance the characterisation of the face.

Towards the end of the 1630's, Rembrandt was showing a better psychological understanding of what the face revealed of the thoughts of a sitter, without any loss in the objective realism. Light effects were improving and harsh contrasts had been eliminated. This meant more freedom in the technique, especially in the portraits which were painted for pleasure rather than profit.

Perhaps the most beautiful example of just this type of portrait is that of *Baartjen Maartens* in the Hermitage. This portrait is undated but it would be reasonable to place it very near to that of her husband, *Herman Doomer* (New York, Metropolitan Museum) which is a companion picture and dated 1640. Their son, Lambert Doomer, who was a landscape painter, was a pupil of Rembrandt's at this time, and probably the artist was friendly with the parents. As Herman Doomer was a frame maker it is also quite probable that he had Rembrandt as a customer. Even if we did not know these facts, it could be guessed from her portrait that it was not a commission but a portrait of a friend, and it is also clear that she is an ordinary not an aristocratic person. Rembrandt has brought her to life in a superbly inspired moment of creation. She sits attentively, hands clasped, and is obviously delighted at having her portrait painted. The faint smile of her lips is taken up in the eyes, in the way that only the greatest painters can convey. Yet, if this much is obvious, much more is suggested by her delicate gentle face. The eyes look out and yet are also turned inwards to her own personal thoughts—a perfect balance of outward and inward expression in a portrait. The light flows around the face, casting a warm shadow on the cool white ruff, which itself reflects white light up on to her chin. In the breadth of handling, in the beauty of the lighting, and above all in the quiet mood of inward reflection, this portrait of Baartjen Maartens lets us look ahead to what Rembrandt was to achieve in his quarter of a century of portrait painting yet to come.

Plate 5—REMBRANDT VAN RIJN: The Denial of St Peter (detail). Rembrandt's absorption with light naturally led him to use the effects of candlelight or firelight to great

Plate 10. JAN VERMEER (Delft 1632 - 1675):
The Lacemaker. Oil on canvas, 24 x 21 cm (9¹/₂ x 8¹/₄ ins). Paris, Louvre.

Plate 11. JAN VERMEER:
Lady Standing at a Virginal. Oil on canvas, 50 x 45 cm (20¹/₄ x 17³/₄ ins). London, National Gallery.

advantage. Two works of his last years are supreme illustrations of what he could achieve in this way. One of these was an interior scene, *The Conspiracy of Julius Civilis* (Stockholm, National Museum) of 1662, which was referred to in the Introduction, but the other was an outdoor scene, *The Denial of St Peter* of 1660. A preparatory drawing for the *Denial* shows that Rembrandt began with a more elaborate composition with more figures and gesture, but then, as is so often the case in the late masterpieces, he simplified the composition to concentrate on the essentials of the human story. The theme is the familiar one of human weakness. St Peter's expression and hesitant gesture convey to us all the astonished grief he is experiencing. The servant girl holds up a candle, shielded by her hand, to flood the face of the Saint in a warmth of golden orange light that breaks up the faces and garments into simplified, broad masses and planes. The colouring, with the candlelight vibrating on St Peter's white robe and on the red and white clothes of the servant girl, is typical of that richness which came anew to Rembrandt in the 'sixties.

The scene is completed around the dominant figure of St Peter by two soldiers in the foreground, one of whom is seated in front of an unseen fire in the foreground. The firelight plays wondrously on his shining black armour, making a magnificent contrast with the white robe of St Peter. On the right, far in the background, the small figure of Christ, held by his captors, looks back over His shoulder at His disciple who has just denied Him. This background group is actually illuminated by a third source of light, much cooler than the flame-lit drama of the foreground. Rembrandt has united the three groups, with their different lighting, into a unified and effective composition, painted with the masterly freedom that makes *The Denial of St Peter* an exciting work of art as well as a deeply moving story.

Plate 6—HERCULES SEGHERS: Landscape or Great Mountain View. Hercules Seghers owes his present recognition as a painter to the perception of a great art historian. At Florence in 1871, Wilhelm von Bode made the first of his many notable contributions to art history by putting forward the view that a large landscape painting in the Uffizi Gallery was not by Rembrandt, to whom it had always been attributed, but by Hercules Seghers. Although his etchings, about seventy in number, were then known, it was the first painting by Seghers to be recognised. After this discovery a slow investigation of Seghers began, which has only gathered momentum in the last forty years. Four paintings bearing a signature or monogram have now come to light, and on this basis it has been possible to attribute more paintings to him which had previously been wrongly attributed to other artists. The known group of paintings is being increased by the occasional discovery of more landscapes, especially in England where they had been bought as Rembrandt's originally — this was the case with the Uffizi picture called the *Great Mountain View*. A document exists of 1631 recording the sale of his house in Amsterdam, and at the same time he sold about seventy paintings to a dealer. Thus it is probable that more paintings still exist and will continue to be found. This comparatively recent discovery of Seghers and the importance of his work has led to an enormous rise in the value of his paintings and etchings —a single etching was recently sold for over L 12,000. In this enthusiasm for a newly discovered artist, a large number of paintings have been wrongly attributed to him, and these errors, in addition to the genuine lack of information about his life, have led to a confused image of Seghers. From the few available facts it is clear that during an early journey to the Alps he made etchings of mountain landscapes. He probably painted pictures from these, after he had settled in Amsterdam, but also continued etching and making pioneer experiments with colour printing of etchings and other methods of heightening the effectiveness of the medium. He seems to have been successful, and was prosperous from about 1615 to the end of the 1620's, after which his popularity declined. Seghers became an isolated figure, falling into considerable debt and poverty at the time of his death.

Faced with this absence of factual information (there are, for example, no dated works) our high estimation of Seghers' stature can only be based on his work.

The *Great Mountain View* in the Uffizi Gallery is the largest and finest known painting by Hercules Seghers. Although undated, it may belong to the later 1620's. It is a perfect example of his achievement, combining all the elements of his art. The panoramic view, the scale of the figures, the atmospheric cloud effects, the superb colours amid the general monochrome, are all typical of Seghers' paintings. He combines a distant and accurate view of a Dutch town in the background with the valley and precipices of an Alpine landscape. A majestic conception, filled with the awesome power of nature, is brought to life by accuracy of detail, mood, and lighting. The original attribution to Rembrandt was not without foundation. It is practically certain that it was among the eight paintings by Seghers that Rembrandt owned, and that Rembrandt made alterations to it. No greater compliment could have been paid to Seghers than the intense interest in him shown by Rembrandt, and the influence of Seghers is clearly seen in Rembrandt's landscapes. Seghers represents a unique merging of the 'world landscape' of the sixteenth century with the most advanced style of seventeenth-century Dutch landscape painting. He remains today a strange figure whose highly personal style and spiritual intensity leave us as bewildered as we are impressed.

Plate 7—PIETER SAENREDAM: St James, Utrecht.

Pieter Saenredam is one of the most original and individual figures in the history of Dutch painting. There is high praise today for any signs of creative originality in artists, and we would be mistaken to let Saenredam's limited subject matter blind us to his unprecedented achievements with church interiors.

Like so many of the true innovators in Dutch painting, Saenredam worked in Haarlem. After a training in the conventional methods and subject matter of academic painting under Peter de Grebber, he turned to the church interior and the architectural view and found there a subject of lifelong fascination. He may have been helped in this direction by his friendship with the famous architect Jacob van Campen. In dealing with his treatment of church interiors, it must be remembered that Protestant churches were very austere and plain—there are few recorded commissions for religious paintings to be placed in churches. Thus, in many cases, Saenredam was not, in fact, exaggerating the blank and sparsely furnished appearance of the church. He developed from the 1620's an increasingly wide and subtle range of colours and tones, together with an exquisite sensitivity to the fall of light through the church windows. He possessed also the sense of perspective and detailed finish which were essential to his approach. Within a limited possible use of colour he found an infinite variation of tone. Sunlight floods onto one wall, casting a transparent shadow on the opposite walls, which become three or four shades darker than the white or cream colour where the direct light falls. It is in the merging and interplay of the two extremes of light and shadow that he took such pains to be accurate in tone. A typical scene might be a church with creamy stonework, light brown, yellowish woodwork in the roof and pews, above a pale grey-green stone floor. Another picture might be quite different with pinky-brown walls, a blue-grey shiny floor, and pale blue sky seen through the windows. Though it seems that Saenredam, in the 'twenties, can be seen within the era of 'tonal painting', he rapidly developed a sense of light colour, pure white in particular, which seemed to anticipate the ideals of the Delft School.

The exhibition devoted to Saenredam in 1961 brought him greater popularity than ever before. One of the reasons for this appeal to modern taste lies in the most intriguing aspect of his art—the abstract qualities of all his pictures. The superb feeling for abstract values makes itself immediately felt in his work, and develops together with his other qualities. Seen in this way, his interior of a church suddenly becomes a stimulating and complex study of line and mass, and of their relationship one to another. The accents are provided by the small dark figures or the rectangular and diamond-shaped shields hanging on a pillar, or the different colours of the tiles and tombstones in the floor. Nothing in Dutch art was comparable to this abstract beauty until Piet Mondrian developed his final style during the First World War.

The *Interior of St. James' Church at Utrecht* (Munich, Alte Pinakothek) of 1642 shows not only all these facets of Saenredam's art, but gains something extra from the composition —an intriguing close-up with a single figure of a man and his dog. The high vaults allow a very complex play of light and shadow. As in so many Dutch paintings, here is the real subject matter of the picture—the mystery of the light. It gives the plasticity to the vast columns, and creates the realistic impression of light and atmosphere that fills the quiet corner of the church. Saenredam also painted exteriors with the same beautiful details and clean lines, and the same deceptive simplicity.

An outstanding example of this type of exterior scene is the *View of the Old Town Hall* (Amsterdam, Rijksmuseum) of 1657—a picture in the finest possible condition, with a quality surpassing the highest aspirations of Van der Heyden (*see* Introduction).

Saenredam's competitors and pupils profited from his popularising of the church interior, but they could never achieve the purity of colour and composition that made Pieter Saenredam a genius in his own field.

Plate 8—GABRIEL METSU: A Woman seated at a Table and a Man tuning a Violin. Gabriel Metsu was a remarkably prolific artist whose early death was to some extent offset by the precocious start of his career. The chronology of his work and the origins of his style are not clearly understood, but the attractions of his paintings need no explanation. In Leyden, he was a pupil of one of Rembrandt's earliest followers, Gerrit Dou, and a friend of Jan Steen. By 1648 Metsu had gained a sufficient reputation to be a founder member of the Guild, although only nineteen years old. He moved from Leyden and eventually settled in Amsterdam in 1657, where he married and lived a prosperous life until illness caused his death in 1667.

From the bare facts of his life, one could expect to see something of the Rembrandtesque, the gusto of Steen, and the intimacy of Dou, all of which are in fact present in his work. Metsu was a highly sensitive artist who absorbed different influences and formed an art of his own. Until the mid-'fifties he painted religious subjects as well as everyday scenes, such as *The Smithy* (London, National Gallery). After he had moved to Amsterdam, undoubtedly influenced by what was most in demand, he tended to concentrate on genre scenes. Two figures in an elegant interior engaged in some pleasant occupation would be typical—for example, the *Woman seated at a Table and a Man tuning a Violin*, in the National Gallery, London. In this mature work, which probably dates from the early 'sixties, the treatment of the background in warm browns and yellows suggests the knowledge of Rembrandt which has already been mentioned, and the mood created by the two figures has the intimacy of Dou and something of his attention to detail, yet free from his master's sentimentality. In treating this type

of elegant subject, Metsu must have been well aware of the achievement of Terborch (*see* Plate 23 and its Note), but he generally attains a deeper sensitivity to the thoughts and emotions of his subjects. It would be fair to suggest that both Metsu and Terborch gained from the example of each other. Metsu never aimed at the same pitch of perfect finish that characterises Terborch, but he could certainly paint with greater ease. There is an underlying warmth and vitality in Metsu's scenes which suggests that he had not forgotten his early contacts with Jan Steen. His feeling for colour is delightfully illustrated in the harmonies of red, orange and brown which give this picture such radiance. These elegant genre scenes frequently feature a rich Turkish carpet on the table, very much a status symbol, of the prosperity of the great cities in the second half of the seventeenth century. Perhaps the only weakness that Metsu succumbed to was a very understandable one. Endowed with superb fluency and charm of technique, it was natural for him to respond to the demand for his pictures by painting as many as he could. Inevitably the freshness and sparkle of the best of them could not be sustained in all.

Plate 9—PIETER DE HOOGH: The Courtyard of a House in Delft. Pieter de Hoogh will always be compared with Vermeer, just as Frans Hals is with Rembrandt. The comparison is neither particularly damaging nor valuable. It has already been seen that the difference between Delft's two leading painters was no more and no less than the difference between the fine artist and the genius. Although De Hoogh greatly benefited from the example of Vermeer's genius, he was himself an exceptionally gifted and original artist. This reputation rests on a group of only forty pictures, painted during ten years at Delft, the rarity and beauty of which has made them the treasured and unobtainable possessions of a few fortunate museums and private collections. Of these, perhaps no picture is a better example of De Hoogh's gift than *The Courtyard of a House in Delft*, in the National Gallery, London. This is a painting whose condition is little short of miraculous after three centuries, and its universal appeal has made it a favourite subject for reproduction. The perfect balance of the composition emphasises the strongly architec-

Plate 12. NICHOLAES MAES
(Dordrecht 1634 - Amsterdam 1693):
Girl at a Window (detail). Oil on panel.
Amsterdam, Rijksmuseum.

Plate 13. ADRIAEN BROUWER
(Oudenarde 1605/6 - Antwerp 1638):
The Smoker. Oil on panel, 29 x 20 cm (11⁸/₄ x 8¹/₄ ins).
Amsterdam, Rijksmuseum.

tural quality of both De Hoogh's outdoor scenes and his interiors. One is forcefully reminded of the abstract construction of Saenredam. The apparently natural appearance of the courtyard is, in reality, a study of line and shape where the placing of every object has the deliberation of a great still-life painter. The flat shapes of open doors, the diagonal of a broom, the cylinder of a bucket, the patterning of paving and brickwork, all contribute to the complex of shape and colour. However, if this is the intellectual appeal of *The Courtyard*, it is subordinated to the feeling of happy domestic life which was the background of the artist himself and which is so strongly reflected in all his pictures.

This outdoor scene is brought to life by that use of pure bright daylight which is the keynote of the Delft School. Light effects are greatly enhanced by the white stonework in the walls and corridors and in the crumbling plaster that sticks to the brickwork on the right. The house and its courtyard are not fanciful images but the real thing; there are many such houses in Delft which have remained largely unaltered to the present day.

The same principles of construction and space definition apply equally to his interior scenes—for example, *The Interior of a Dutch House* of 1658 (London, National Gallery). In particular, the black and white tiles of the floor diminish into the distance in a most convincing and mathematically correct way. Even away from the bright sunlight, the local colours are strong and rich in variety. The sunlight streaming through the window is gradually diffused across the room where the long shadows of the figures by the window fall across the tiles. The picture's spirit is again one of secure domestic homeliness which typifies the life of the Dutch people.

The decline of Pieter de Hoogh during the last twenty years of his life has been exaggerated. In Amsterdam he was forced to cater for the desire of the wealthy upper classes to be portrayed at leisured amusements in the splendour of their lavish houses. A typical picture of these later years is a musical party where beautifully dressed ladies delight elegant men with their music. The lighting became more subdued and with it the strength of colour, but De Hoogh, who could never become a bad painter, retained a sense of composition and atmosphere which gives quality even to this neglected period.

Plate 10—JAN VERMEER: The Lacemaker. It is very probable that if some of the old dirt and varnish were removed from the smallest of Jan Vermeer's paintings, *The Lacemaker* in the Louvre, it would prove even more 'jewel-like' than it has so often been described. Even in its present mellowed condition it appears like a miraculous close-up of one of Vermeer's typical young girls at work. Here is the favourite harmony of blue, yellow and white, augmented by the brilliant threads of colour which spill out of the work basket. The subject is absorbed in concentration on her intricate task, unconcerned with the gaze of the spectator. As Vermeer's father was a silk merchant, the artist was probably very familiar with this subject. He has treated it with the utmost objectivity, striving, as always, for the perfect illusion of reality.

The Lacemaker is like a still life where the artist has lingered over the exact representation of different textures; the value of each surface, whether it is the chunky pile of the rug, the smooth solidity of the wood, the crinkling folds of the silk, or the transparent surface of the skin, is conveyed to the full and united by the perfectly observed fall of light. Yet, unlike a still life, the whole picture has the feeling of a single moment of time, captured with an inspired spontaneity. This feeling is obviously most strongly conveyed by the poised hands of the lacemaker as she gently draws up the bobbins.

Considering the size of the picture, which is actually smaller than the reproduction, it has a compelling effect on the spectator which is unique even in the work of Jan Vermeer.

Plate 11—JAN VERMEER: Lady Standing at a Virginal. By contrast to the 'close-up' feeling of *The Lacemaker*, Vermeer's *Lady Standing at a Virginal* (London, National Gallery) is a complete composition. It is a work of about 1670, when Vermeer had achieved perfection in his search for truth and beauty. The composition has the ultimate refinement of symmetry and geometric construction, where every shape plays its subtle, unnoticed part. The painting of Cupid appears in its decorative and 'geometric' role in several pictures, but here the proportion and shape are particularly well related to the shape of the picture itself. We do not know whether this studio prop, hardly a great work of art, was also meant to

Plate 14. ADRIAEN VAN OSTADE (Haarlem 1610 - 1685):
A Peasant Courting an Elderly Woman. Oil on panel, 27 x 21 cm (10³/₄ x 8³/₄ ins). London, National Gallery.

Plate 15. JACOB VAN RUISDAEL (Haarlem 1628/9 - Amsterdam 1682):
Landscape. Oil on canvas, 61 x 61 cm (24¹/₂ x 24¹/₂ ins). Madrid, Prado.

suggest a romantic atmosphere or symbolise some happy event in the life of the attractive musician. She looks up from her playing with the same dreamy, thoughtful expression that Vermeer gave to her as a letter writer; for all Vermeer's young ladies, whatever is engaging their attention, share the same inner contentment, full of mysterious and womanly charm.

The colours, clearly very similar to those of *The Lacemaker*, have that 'distilled' purity, seen against the mellow white of the wall, that defies adequate description. Even the wall has been brought to life with the most exacting study of the different tones as the light falls across it. The Delft tiles, which were then such a new and exciting innovation (a skill gained from Holland's East Indian colonies) are as much in evidence today as they were when this delicate masterpiece was being painted. It is as well to remind oneself that it is a picture painted on a flat canvas, so convincing is Vermeer's magical sense of reality. The same foundation of precise geometric construction underlies Vermeer's compositions as it does those of Saenredam and de Hoogh (*see* Note on Plate 7). The history of this late masterpiece of Vermeer also presents an interesting commentary on the development of artistic appreciation, for it was actually sold in a London sale of 1855 for fourteen and a half guineas.

Plate 12—NICHOLAES MAES: Girl at a Window. The story of Nicholaes Maes is the most unusual one of any Dutch artist of the seventeenth century. It also presented the most difficult problems to twentieth-century art historians.

Maes entered the Rembrandt studio in 1648 as a very young pupil. He soon proved himself not only a competent painter but an artist capable of understanding the qualities of his master. Under Rembrandt's influence, Maes painted, in the years from the early 1650's to the mid 'sixties, genre pictures of great beauty. He employed Rembrandt's chiaroscuro and warmth of colour in domestic scenes of great charm, often with a single figure quietly engaged in an everyday task. The settings are usually carefully depicted, giving a convincing atmosphere and realism to the scene. One of the most poetic and beautiful pictures of this kind is the *Old Woman saying Grace* (Amsterdam, Rijksmuseum). In such pictures,

Maes seems also to have learnt from Pieter de Hoogh, his sincere belief in the essential goodness of tranquil domestic life.

At the same time as the *Old Woman saying Grace*, Maes painted what is, perhaps, his most attractive work of all, the *Girl at a Window* (Amsterdam, Rijksmuseum). The appeal of this girl, lost in reflection, is irresistible, and has led to the picture often being called simply 'Dreaming.' The mood of contemplation, the gaze turned away from the spectator, brings Vermeer strongly to mind—the relationship between the two artists is not clear but they cannot have been unaware of each other. The bright red of her turban is the favourite colour of Maes, and is seen in most of his pictures. In this one it is used in a slightly lighter shade in the shutter of the window, which is not shown here, and, of course, in the rug. Though this colour derives from Rembrandt, Maes found a particular shade of his own, and used it in a very personal way. The large scale of the figure, compared to the setting, is characteristic of Maes, and here gives 'the Dreamer' great presence. Apart from the scale of the figure, the type of subject and the general composition must depend on Rembrandt's example in the *Girl at a Doorway* of 1645 (Chicago, Art Institute). The most serious limitation in the style of Maes, which a comparison of the two brings out, is his relatively restricted type of handling. He cannot produce sufficient variations of brushwork to give the different textures their full value. Yet, whatever his understandable limitations compared with his great teacher, the Maes of this period possessed something of Rembrandt's supreme poetry, whose influence is nowhere better seen than in the *Girl at a Window*.

Apparently not content with painting in this manner, Maes made a journey to Antwerp in the mid 1660's and studied the Flemish masters. He had already begun to paint portraits in Amsterdam and may have wanted to improve them by studying, at first hand, the work of Van Dyck. Whatever the explanation, his style was completely changed after his return to Amsterdam. So startling is the difference between the early and later work that they were at one time thought to be the work of two different artists of the same name. The later one was, significantly, called the 'Brussels Maes.' He abandoned the last vestiges of the Rembrandtesque, and catered to the demand for bust-length fashionable portraits of the gentry. He was very successful and these late portraits are as numerous as they are insignificant. The fame of Nicholaes Maes rests on that comparatively brief period when he so sympathetically interpreted the teaching of Rembrandt.

Plate 13—ADRIAEN BROUWER: The Smoker.

Adriaen Brouwer spent his career as much in Holland as in his native Flanders, —consequently he is claimed by both schools. The eagerness of these claims arises from his unique importance in the story of genre painting. The content of these seventeenth-century low life genre scenes sometimes offends present-day tastes, but they must be looked at within the context of their age. To allow the subject matter—the drunken, brawling peasants —to blind one to the artistic qualities of these paintings is a sad mistake, above all in the case of Adriaen Brouwer, the greatest artist of the genre.

Information about his short, vivid existence is unfortunately fragmentary. Yet the known facts are even more intriguing than the many lurid but imagined stories about Brouwer, and form an essential background to his work. At the age of sixteen he ran away from home to the northern provinces. He is mentioned in 1626 as a member of a literary society in Amsterdam, and described as 'far famed'. It is probable that he spent the early years of the 1620's in Frans Hals' studio and then built up this reputation in Amsterdam. There is then a complete gap from 1627 to 1631. He is recorded as being in Antwerp in 1631, and remained there until his death in 1638, at the age of thirty-three. No proof is known of the legend that he was killed in a tavern fight. A document of 1632 exists in which he testified that he had not painted any other version of a ' Kermesse ' (Fair) which belonged to Rubens—the picture is now lost. In the following year, an inventory of his possessions was made. It showed him to be poor in normal possessions, but the owner of a Joos van Cleeve painting, two landscapes by de Momper, an older, contemporary Flemish artist, and no less than eight books, which were rare and expensive items at that time. The inventory also included a map of the Siege of Breda, 1625-6, and it has been suggested that Brouwer may have taken part in this siege on the Dutch side. He was imprisoned in the Spanish Fortress at Antwerp in 1633. Now the Fortress was used for political prisoners, not the ordinary civil offenders who went to the town gaol. We can only guess what Brouwer's political offence was, and whether it was connected with the Siege of Breda. The Fortress housed shops and a tavern for the Spanish soldiers who were not popular in the city. It was to this miniature community that Brouwer was confined.

During his time in prison, he ran up a considerable debt which was then settled by his main patron, Den Basch. In return, the artist agreed to paint for him a hundred florins' worth of paintings per month. In 1634, Brouwer went to live with an engraver called Pontius, and through him met a wide circle of people. He again joined a literary circle. The remaining few years of his life were the most productive but as most of the pictures were painted for creditors they did not appear on the open market, and those which did consequently brought unusually high prices. Rubens must have therefore taken some trouble to acquire the seventeen paintings by Brouwer which he possessed. Equally so Rembrandt, who owned eight Brouwers. Even in these years of living in respectable circles, Brouwer became so indebted to the local tavern owner that he was forced to give him his Van Cleeve and a Van Dyck painting—what debts these would settle today! Brouwer was buried very rapidly after his death, which suggests that he died of the plague. Many distinguished artists were among the mourners when he was re-buried in a church.

From these known facts, several things are clear. Brouwer was an educated and literary-minded man whose work was admired by the greatest contemporary artists. Van Dyck's engraved portrait of him, an aristocratic and sensitive face, bears out this assessment. That he was given to frequenting taverns, where he enjoyed smoking and drinking a good deal, cannot be doubted, but he was not of the same mould as the company it amused him to keep. In a short life, not by any means devoted exclusively to painting, he did not produce many pictures, and genuine works of his are rare today. His paintings are all on a small scale, all on panel, and not one is dated. His early pictures were generally executed in bright colours, with a strong element of caricature. These have understandably been catalogued as School of Brueghel. His bright Flemish colours must

Plate 16. MEINDERT HOBBEMA (Amsterdam 1638 - 1709):
The Ruins of Brederode Castle. Oil on canvas, 82 x 106 cm (32¹/₄ x 41³/₄ ins). London, National Gallery.

Plate 17. JAN VAN GOYEN (Leyden 1596 - The Hague 1656):
View of Dordrecht. Oil on panel, 55 x 72 cm (22 x 28³/₄ ins). Amsterdam, Rijksmuseum.

have been unfamiliar in Haarlem, but he combined them with a Dutch feeling for light and shadow. This applies also to the fifteen landscapes which it is surprising to find he painted. By the later 1620's his work became far more refined in draughtsmanship and execution, his colours more beautiful, and his compositions more ordered. Brouwer somehow brought the dexterity and forcefulness of Hals' technique to his small, exquisitely painted panels. The dramatic concentration of figures or the momentary attitude of a single figure called for observation and draughtsmanship of the highest order. These small scenes were cabinet pictures which collectors could hold in their hands to admire for the finish and surface quality. The subjects were amusing and often had an allegorical or moral lesson implied, but the beauty of the painting was their value in the eyes of a class of collectors far removed from anything so vulgar as a tavern.

The Smoker (Amsterdam, Rijksmuseum) illustrates all Brouwer's qualities of brushwork and colour, together with the atmosphere which has already been stressed. It reveals at the same time an important essential of his work, the structure. These apparently casual compositions are, in fact, most carefully built up with the same knowledge and care as those of an abstract painter. Squares, rectangles, triangles and circles are all there and all perfectly related. This structure brings harmony, balance and depth to all Brouwer's pictures. Whatever our reaction to Brouwer's manner of living and choice of subject, everyone should grasp the outstanding artistic merit of this very strange and short-lived painter.

Plate 14 — ADRIAEN VAN OSTADE : A Peasant Courting an Elderly Woman.
Adriaen van Ostade is rightly claimed to be the most productive and well-known painter of the peasantry. One of the remarkable things about painting in seventeenth-century Holland was the democratic range of its enthusiasts. Ownership of paintings was not the privilege of the wealthy or educated, but a reality for all levels of society. Brouwer's career had been too short and unproductive to supply the huge demand for paintings of peasant genre, though he was obviously a giant among his contemporaries, including Ostade. The latter was a more conventional artist whose life had all the regularity that Brouwer's clearly lacked. Ostade remained in Haarlem throughout his long life, which was peaceful and uneventful, and rarely travelled away from his native city. He gradually rose to be Dean of the painters' Guild in 1661.

Ostade's contact with Brouwer, who was his senior by a few years, seems to have influenced the style of his early works. However, there were two distinctive features at the outset of his career. Firstly, his choice of cool pale colours was unlike the stronger palette of Brouwer. Secondly, he showed a preference for large interiors with light falling from a single source, a high window or opening in the roof, leaving a part of the setting in semi-darkness. The influence of Rembrandt's warm brown is apparent in the monochrome style of many of these interior scenes. Ostade was gifted with a fluent style and these pictures are generally executed with great skill. From the 1640's onwards his range of subjects developed, and the whole of his work became calmer with more form to the figures, and a general return of local colours, seen in brighter light. It was in this later style that he painted many of his best known pictures, always humorous but never mocking. We gain a fairly accurate idea of the different aspects of a simple, unaffected way of life which centred on the tavern gatherings (not at all unlike the lives of many hard-working people today). During the 1650's and 1660's, Ostade found his happiest solution of colour and composition, his subject matter excluding much of the coarseness of the early period. He made frequent use of the triangle as a compositional device for the attitude of individual figures and groups. Ostade was essentially a gifted artist and a fine draughtsman, who, like Van Goyen in landscape, supplied a vast demand for his work, which has even today retained much of its popularity. The career of his brother, Isaac van Ostade (1621-1649), was as tragically short as Adriaen's was long and productive. Isaac specialised in open-air genre scenes, always painted with a refinement and detail that is distinctive and, in some ways, superior to his brother's surfaces.

A thoroughly typical example of Adriaen Ostade's work, painted at his best period, is the *Peasant Courting an Elderly Woman*, in the National Gallery, London, which is signed and dated 1653. Like many of his contemporaries, Ostade was able to paint with great ease on the smooth surface of a small oak panel, the colour of the wood showing through in many places, giving warmth and transparency to the whole surface of the picture so that nothing is allowed to go dully opaque. The man's outline is an example of his use of triangular forms. Though this is a particularly appealing little episode, the surface of the picture is a little worn, robbing us of some of the beauty of the paint surface.

The range and quality of peasant genre painting in Holland and Flanders had no parallel in any other country in the seventeenth century.

Plate 15—JACOB VAN RUISDAEL: Landscape.

Jacob van Ruisdael plays a dominant role in the history of Dutch landscape painting, as emphasised in the Introduction. It is difficult, in looking at reproductions of his paintings, to gain an adequate impression of the quality of the paint surface, or to feel the forcefulness of their mood. The word most frequently used to describe the mood and scale of his pictures is 'heroic', which may sometimes be misleading. There is about them the spirit of an epic tragedy that is governed by the forces of nature. Ruisdael is, of course, best known and recognised for his painting of individual trees, swayed majestically or violently against a menacing sky, and his ability to evoke the sense of impenetrable mystery of forests. The woodland subjects are in a sense less Dutch, less typical of the landscape achievements of the whole school, than the smaller views of towns or the superb winter scenes. So prolific was the artist that many museums have a selection of his work which shows its different aspects. This enables the visitor to see the difference between the Ruisdael of the small-scale view, for example the very fine *View of Haarlem* seen across the bleaching grounds (Amsterdam, Rijksmuseum), and the Ruisdael of the great oaks and forests, of which the painting illustrated is typical. Ruisdael leads the eye along rough paths between towering trees, probing with great realism into the shadows of a forest that borders on the edge of a lake. The mood of storm and gloomy unrest suggested by the trees is greatly enhanced by the magnificent sky, where pale yellows and pinks mark the breaks in the steely blue-grey clouds. Where light breaks through the clouds, it falls in patches of strangely bright colouring in the foliage and on the trunks of the trees. All this is so accurately observed that the effect is powerfully convincing. This work emphasises the most important aspect of Ruisdael's work, his feeling for the true structure of a landscape. He was an artist who thoroughly understood what he was painting. It was a knowledge acquired through years of devoted study and application. His rich, deep colour and effective use of impasto strengthen the feeling of solidity and realism for which this sense of structure is so very important. Inevitably, these qualities made Ruisdael the most influential artist of the Dutch School for eighteenth-century landscape painting. He was too profound and troubled a spirit to produce the tranquil, happy landscapes which were the creations of most Dutch painters. Like Rembrandt, Jacob Ruisdael was able to convey in his work as a painter the deepest of his emotions as a man.

Plate 16—MEINDERT HOBBEMA: The Ruins of Brederode Castle.

Meindert Hobbema was a giant among the weak group of Ruisdael's followers. He undoubtedly spent a considerable period of time with Ruisdael, with whom he enjoyed a close friendship.

From Ruisdael he learnt the importance of composition and detail, but he somehow remained unaffected by the epic mood of his teacher's landscapes. The work of Hobbema is self-consciously pretty, which is the last adjective one would apply to Ruisdael.

At the start of Hobbema's career, Ruisdael's example was in a sense an overpowering influence, and it is only gradually that the natural talents of Hobbema appear. His palette became slightly artificial in a way that no doubt impressed later French landscape painters in the eighteenth century. A mixture of light green and grey is the characteristic colour which distinguishes Hobbema's foliage, and he frequently uses dabs and dots of bright colour, such as a rust red or blue-green, to pick out the moss on tree trunks and branches. This colour scheme gives a brightness and clarity to his best pictures that, together with his fine brushwork and sense of detail, place his landscapes among the most pleasing creations of the whole movement. The freshness of these pictures may partly derive from the conditions under which he was working. In 1668 he married a maidservant of one of the Burgomasters of Amsterdam.

Plate 18. AERT VAN DER NEER (Amsterdam 1603/4 - 1677):
The Big Moonlight Scene. Oil on panel, 55 x 103 cm (22 x 41¹/₄ ins). Amsterdam, Rijksmuseum.

Plate 19. JAN VAN DE CAPELLE (Amsterdam c. 1624 - 1679):
The State Barge Saluted by the Home Fleet (detail). Oil on panel. Amsterdam, Rijksmuseum.

He obtained, through a friend of his new wife, a minor post as a 'wine-gauger' in the customs, which provided him with a living. Thus Hobbema was free to paint as a pleasurable hobby rather than to earn a living or fulfil a commission. Yet freed of these restrictions, he did not make any new experiments in composition or colouring and continued painting variations of a single subject, or even actual repetitions of it. His favourite subject of a mill in a forest with a stream splashing over the mill wheel was repeated so often that it is difficult to look at a version of it impartially. By contrast, in moments of inspiration he created new and important compositions, of which the most famous is undoubtedly *The Avenue at Middelharnis* — a wonderful picture that was an inspiration to Sisley and many others.

A picture of considerable beauty, though not as inspired as the *Avenue*, is *The Ruins of Brederode Castle*, in the National Gallery, London, which is signed and dated 1671. It is typical of Hobbema's layout.

The view is framed by trees on either side and a fallen one in the foreground, with a stream or path leading the eye into the distance. There is here, however, a more than average sense of realism due to the appearance of the ruins, which are accurately observed (they are of much the same appearance today). Hobbema, like Ruisdael, is largely unconcerned with figures, and not even capable of painting them with any skill—those in this picture, together with the rather charming geese, were added by another artist. The whole scene is refreshingly open and simple compared to his scenes of dense forests where only a small cottage is seen nestling among the trees. The colouring, with the subtle ranges of green, the blues in the water and landscape, and the reddish stonework, which is so well reflected in the foreground, is typical of this highly gifted but unambitious artist.

Hobbema had a considerable influence on the English landscape painters, and his pictures have always held a great appeal for English collectors.

Plate 17—JAN VAN GOYEN: View of Dordrecht. Recognition of the true position of Jan Van Goyen has come about only within the last forty years. From the status of a lesser master he has come to be regarded, quite correctly, as one of the most important Dutch landscape painters.

He began his studies at the unusually early age of ten, but the accounts of his beginnings are confused, as he seems to have had several minor figures for teachers. In 1615 he went on a prolonged journey in France and may have lived there for a short period. After his return he spent an important year in Haarlem with Esias van de Velde, whose style dominated Van Goyen's work until the late 1620's. In 1618 he married and moved to Leyden, where he lived until the early 1630's, when he moved to The Hague, remaining there until his death.

There is no indication of what Van Goyen's style was before his earliest dated picture of 1620, which shows the dominating influence of Esias van de Velde. These early pictures of the 1620's are brightly coloured with a rather weak arrangement of traditional motifs, and lively groups of figures crowding the foreground. In the 1630's his approach quickly became more realistic. Dune landscapes and coast scenes, very similar to those of a Haarlem painter, Pieter Molijn, became his preoccupation to the exclusion of genre subjects. The sky loses the appearance of a blue backdrop and becomes more related to the ground, with the horizon lowered to give the sky a bigger role in the picture. At the same time, local colours gradually give way to a dominant yellow and green monochrome effect. The compositions, though still strongly reliant on the diagonal, become a little more natural. In the 'forties Van Goyen changed again to a monochrome palette of brown, golden yellow, or variations of grey-green and grey-blue. He achieved a convincing horizon level and sense of recession, with the compositions becoming more open where sky and sea merge in a realistic haze. In the 1640's Van Goyen achieved an accuracy of description and tonal value which is remarkable to anyone familiar with the nature of Holland's landscape. He was able to give the vast skies of estuary scenes a feeling of tranquillity and atmospheric truth which anticipated the achievements of many artists two hundred years after his death. It is instructive to follow his development in some detail, as it occupies a central position in the development of Dutch landscape as a whole. In his last ten years he began to re-introduce local colour into the monochrome style. Yet his monochrome palette of the 1640's had so many fine variations of a single shade that he created a sense of 'colour' without using the normal pigments. His brushwork reached its maximum freedom in the 1640's, when his brush literally drew into the wet paint, sweeping over the barely primed oak panel with great rapidity. Van Goyen was a tireless painter and draughtsman whose output was prodigious. He travelled throughout Holland and visited the southern Netherlands and Germany, apart from the early journey to France. As a successful artist he was reasonably prosperous, but his financial speculating in bulbs led him into considerable debt and he probably painted his way out of it.

The *View of Dordrecht* (Amsterdam, Rijksmuseum) is a mature work, typical of the style and format I have described. The boats and buildings are always placed to give a very effective sense of recession. It is misleading to imagine, in speaking of realistic landscape, that artists like Van Goyen painted exactly what they saw. A sense of artistic composition is always present, but in the sky and lighting he certainly did aim at exact representation. Van Goyes'n position in the history of landscape painting is secure. His pictures, once thought to be innumerable, are gradually becoming unobtainable to those who, like the people of seventeenth-century Holland, enjoy having a poetic and beautiful landscape in their home.

Plate 18—AERT VAN DER NEER: The Big Moonlight Scene. Aert van der Neer was perhaps the most accomplished 'specialist' Dutch landscape painter. If Van Goyen was the painter of the typical Dutch scene, Van der Neer was the seeker after the more mysterious aspects of nature. He was something of an amateur painter, but none the less devoted to his art. As the steward of a wealthy family in his early years, he had no need to paint for a living. However, in the 1630's he did try to establish himself as an artist in Amsterdam and began painting regularly. The earliest dated work is of 1634. The appeal of his winter landscapes and moonlight scenes seems to have been considerable, yet he had difficulty in selling them for anything but the smallest sums of money. In the late 1650's and early 1660's he kept an inn to try to make a living, but even this venture was unsuccessful. Van der Neer shared the fate of many of the most talented Dutch artists in that he died

in great poverty and the pictures left in his studio were sold off for practically nothing. Though it is not recorded who taught him to paint, it seems likely that he had a knowledge of the palette of the Rubens style of landscape, at least, which would explain the warmth of colour in many of his pictures. Van der Neer is probably best known as the painter of moonlight, but many of his pictures were devoted to the light of dawn and dusk as well, and he painted winter scenes which are comparable in quality with those of Jacob van Ruisdael and Van de Capelle. His compositions are generally very similar: an expanse of calm water in the centre flanked by trees and houses with figures on a path in the foreground. These views were studio creations devised without relation to any actual topographical view. Van der Neer is criticised for his monotonous repetition of the same, rather archaic, composition, but it must be remembered that he was absorbed with the study of the many secrets of light. It was relatively unimportant to him what the light was falling on. He understood equally well the quality of cold grey light falling from a leaden sky on to snow or a frozen river where skaters animated the scene, or the warmth of a sunset flooding a landscape with red and golden rays in Claude-like fashion, or the pale watery mists of the full moon. Even this variety was not the limit of his interest. When a great fire broke out in Amsterdam, Van der Neer had to work with great speed to capture on canvas the fascinating effects of firelight.

Of the moonlight pictures, one of the best is *The Big Moonlight Scene* (Amsterdam, Rijksmuseum). It has a striking contrast between the pale coolness of moonlight and the warm browns of the path and houses. Until the time of the Impressionists, no painter gave such a rendering of this very complex subject. Van der Neer must be placed among that group of artists who reached perfection in their chosen subject. Alas, in his own lifetime it proved to be an unrewarded achievement.

Plate 19—JAN VAN DE CAPELLE: The State Barge Saluted by the Home Fleet. Jan van de Capelle ranks second only to Willem van de Velde the Younger, as the greatest marine artist of the Dutch School. In the seventeenth century, not only the economic life but the military strength of the Dutch

Plate 20. PHILIPS WOUWERMANS (Haarlem 1619 - 1668):
The Executioner's House. Oil on canvas, 56 x 68.5 cm (22¹/₄ x 26 ins). Dresden, Gemäldegalerie.

republic depended on the abilities of her sea-farers. The Dutch people had a natural interest in the sea and ships, and they thoroughly understood the importance of the sea to their country. Holland's navy had played the same role against the Spaniards that the British navy was to play against Napoleon—in both cases ultimate victory depending on sea power.

One of the founders of Dutch marine painting was Hendrik Cornelisz. Vroom who worked, like so many pioneers of Dutch painting, in Haarlem. It was the experience of being shipwrecked that, far from giving him a lasting fear of the sea, turned him from landscape and genre painting to a study of ships and the sea. Naturally, the early marine artists were bound by conventions and formulas similar to those of the landscape painters. In the next generation, two artists in particular brought marine painting forward to the same sense of realism as had been achieved in landscape. One of these artists was Jan Porcellis (c. 1584-1632), a pupil of Hendrik Vroom, whose work is characterised by an interest in stormy seas and dark cloudy skies. Porcellis was not a sufficiently inventive artist to change, during his career, the style of his early pictures. By contrast, Simon De Vlieger (1601-1653) might be compared, as an innovator, to Van Goyen. Like most of the important marine painters, De Vlieger's knowledge was soundly based on innumerable drawings of his subject. He was capable of depicting, in a largely monochrome palette, the different moods of the sea with great fidelity to nature.

After the period of transition represented by De Vlieger, the story reaches its most exciting moment with Jan van de Capelle. In several ways he was a unique figure in Dutch painting. His father was the wealthy owner of a dye works and van de Capelle worked in the family business which he eventually inherited. He seems to have begun painting as a pastime at an early age and his boast that he was self-taught is probably accurate. Throughout his life he used his wealth to collect a very large number of paintings and drawings. When an inventory of his collection was drawn up after his death, it showed clearly his appreciation of his important predecessor De Vlieger, for Van de Capelle owned nine paintings and over a thousand drawings of his. The collection also included sixteen paintings by Porcellis, but his interest was by no means limited to marine painting.

He possessed many drawings by Van Goyen, Avercamp, Rembrandt and Hercules Seghers, and examples of the work of many lesser masters. His own work is characterised by a preference for calm seas, which he painted with a deep sense of poetic tranquillity. Van de Capelle rarely showed any interest in the estuary scenes of choppy water that were the favourite subject of De Vlieger and Van Goyen. A perfect example of his exquisite treatment of placid sunlit water is the small panel in the Iveagh Bequest at Kenwood, London. He achieved a merging of the ' tranquil ' estuary scene of Van Goyen with the feeling for sunlight which Cuyp possessed. He also painted about forty very accomplished winter landscapes—a complete contrast to the atmosphere of most of his marine subjects.

The State Barge Saluted by the Home Fleet is one of his most colourful and best-known creations. The detail illustrated here gives us an excellent idea of how perfectly he understood the reflection of light from the flat surface of a calm sea. The large assembly of ships is arranged to give the maximum possible feeling of depth, as the eye is led back into the hazy horizon. It is not known what occasion is represented, or who the important personages were in the State Barge. Although the sky is worn and has lost some of its original beauty, the lower half of the painting remains a truly amazing work by an artist in his twenty-fifth year. It is hard to realise that he considered himself an amateur painter.

Plate 20—PHILIPS WOUWERMANS: The Executioner's House. Philips Wouwermans would be a much more highly regarded artist if he had painted as few pictures as Van de Capelle. His energetic approach and devotion to his work led him to paint more and more pictures. Compositions were repeated and often lost their simplicity as he put large numbers of figures into them. Freshness and quality inevitably suffered. His pictures were popular and he proved himself equal to the demand, although it was clearly to the detriment of his artistic status. At the age of nineteen he eloped to Hamburg but the intended marriage did not take place and he returned within two years to Haarlem. He studied there under Jan Wijnants and possibly Frans Hals, and certainly came into contact with the spirit of the romantic Italian School, through Pieter van Laer. Wouwermans seems

Plate 22. JAN DAVIDZ. DE HEEM (Utrecht 1606 - Antwerp 1684):
Still Life with Books. Oil on panel, 26.5 x 41.5 cm (10¹/₂ x 16¹/₂ ins). Amsterdam, Rijksmuseum.

Plate 21. WILLEM KALF (Rotterdam 1619 - Amsterdam 1693):
Still Life. Oil on canvas, 115 x 86 cm (45 x 34¹/₂ ins). Cologne, Wallraf-Richartz Museum.

to echo throughout his work the effects of this Italianate sentiment, which must have appealed to his apparently romantic character.

Though he was versatile and painted different types of subjects, the great majority of his work was devoted to horsemen in landscapes. Cavalry actions, highway robbers, soldiers in camp, hunting scenes, were his favourite subjects. At his best, Wouwermans was a highly accomplished painter. He must be judged by these superior pictures, where faultless drawing of the horses is complemented by a well-composed landscape, atmospheric and romantic in spirit and the whole picture highly finished. Some of his paintings on copper have a surface quality that would have done credit to artists such as Terborch.

An example of his finest work is *The Executioner's House* (Dresden, Gemäldegalerie; there are, in fact, about sixty pictures by him at Dresden). The landscape has that romantic 'sauvage' quality that immediately brings to mind Salvator Rosa. The agitation in the clouds and in the rapidly flowing stream is echoed by the lively spirit of the group who are breaking their journey to water the horses, among which is the inevitable white horse that is only too well known as his 'signature'. A trivial incident becomes a well-balanced composition, rich in colouring and atmosphere.

Wouwermans' essentially romantic mood was extremely popular with his contemporaries. His cavalry scenes brought back memories of the Thirty Years War, which was already sufficiently long ago to be remembered with enthusiasm in the 1660's. The bare, mountainous landscapes conjured up picturesque visions of a far off country full of romantic adventure. Wouwermans' popularity outlived him by many years, for his works were keenly collected in the eighteenth century, particularly in France.

Plate 21—WILLEM KALF: Still Life. Willem Kalf deserves the highest praise as the greatest exponent of his particular art. He devoted himself to the type of still life, called the 'pronk' (or 'sumptuous') still life at the period, which portrayed different types of fine craftsmanship in metals, glass, and porcelain. The son of a wealthy burgher family in Rotterdam, he remained there until the death of his widowed mother in 1638. He then set out to seek his fortune abroad, and is recorded in 1642 as living in Paris. In 1646 he returned to Holland, and from 1653 onwards he based his career in Amsterdam. Kalf knew his subject matter well enough to be a dealer in metalwork in Amsterdam, and even his wife was well known for her diamond-engraving and calligraphic work. Amsterdam was one of the largest and most wealthy cities in the world. The affluence of her leading society is reflected in their love of the finest creations of goldsmiths and silversmiths, delicate porcelain, Venetian glass, and the most luxurious carpets and rugs. The sumptuousness of Kalf's still lifes seems far removed from the austere 'breakfast pieces' of Heda and Claesz. His subject matter is a fascinating insight into the wealth of Holland in the second half of the seventeenth century.

Even in his twenties he displayed an extraordinary talent for still-life painting. The early works vary from a cool bluish tone to tawny yellows or warm browns. A particularly rich display of craftsmanship is seen in the *Still Life* (Cologne, Wallraf-Richartz Museum), datable in the early 1640's. The tone is one of rich warmth, with the metals given a lustrous and entirely convincing appearance. The space is well defined by the distant background objects and by the device of spreading the display on to a low stool or table in the foreground. Kalf allied his feeling for different textures with a complete grasp of how the light fell on a complex group of shapes. One feels that only an artist who had a first-hand knowledge of the metalsmith's art could have painted the designs on the jugs and salver. In several places he used that pointillist technique, for example in the tassels at the front or in the reflections on the pewter vessel, which characterises his style. He uses it most often for the dots of light catching the peel of a lemon or orange in some of the more simplified compositions, which he turned to in the 1650's. These later works do not possess the vitality and sumptuousness of the kind illustrated here, but they are more profound and poetic, recalling the spirit of the early still-life painters.

It seems unlikely that Kalf continued painting in his later years as the latest dated picture is of 1678, and his output is relatively small. Kalf had superb technical mastery of texture and it was the way he could give life and mood to inanimate objects that allows him to be ranked as a great artist by any standards.

Plate 22—JAN DAVIDZ. DE HEEM: Still Life with Books. Jan de Heem represents, like Kalf, the culmination of achievement in particular types of still life. The history of Dutch still life and flower painting relies on Flanders both at the outset, and in its highpoint, represented by De Heem. At the beginning of the century, Ambrosius Bosschaert came to Holland from his native Flanders to set the pattern, with the help of his sons and other pupils, of flower and fruit painting in the first three decades in Holland. Bosschaert's leading pupil was Balthasar van der Ast, and, as a very young artist in the 1620's, De Heem began working in his style at Utrecht. By 1626 he had moved to Leyden, where he married in that year. After a period of ten years in Leyden he moved to Antwerp where he was admitted to the Guild in 1636. In Antwerp, he learnt from the more elaborate and flamboyant style of the Flemish still-life painters, in particular Frans Snyders and Seghers. Within a few years De Heem was producing very large magnificently executed still lifes combining fruit, flowers and pewter, displayed in palatial surroundings. His work included swags, floral surrounds to portraits, banquet pieces, and many superb pure flower pictures which were initially indebted to the example of the great Jesuit artist, Daniel Seghers. De Heem returned to Utrecht in the 1660's and was in the Guild from 1669 to 1672, but the French invasion forced him back to Antwerp where he stayed until his death. De Heem was soundly trained in his native Holland, but his mastery of the Baroque still life was achieved in Flanders, so that he cannot be claimed to belong solely to either school, but rather represents a synthesis of the two. One of the amazing aspects of his abilities was a fluency of technique which allowed him to paint a very large number of pictures of a high level of quality and finish.

To illustrate the work of this leading artist, a rare early work of his years in Leyden has been chosen in preference to the well-known pictures of his full maturity. It is the *Still Life with Books* of 1628 (Amsterdam, Rijksmuseum). At Leyden, De Heem inevitably felt the influence of Rembrandt's chiaroscuro and of his poetic sincerity. Though it has the elements of a 'Vanitas' picture, De Heem seems more concerned with the objects themselves than with their symbolism. He paints with a greater freedom than most of his contemporaries, and has given the curling pages of the books a very realistic appearance. The lessons he learnt of accuracy in detail and the importance of light and shadow remained very valuable to him when his style changed so completely in Antwerp. It is the beauty of De Heem's flower paintings that often gains the highest praise today. A bouquet of brilliantly coloured flowers in a transparent glass vase is a typical composition. The whole Dutch nation was passionately fond of flowers, particularly the tulip, of which they produced literally hundreds of new varieties in the seventeenth century. The demand was insatiable for the accurate representation of flowers, skilfully arranged, with every drop of water and every tiny insect rendered with the greatest care.

It was the only branch of Dutch painting which was successfully carried on into the eighteenth century by De Heem's two successors, Jan van Huysum, and that most gifted of female artists, Rachel Ruysch.

Plate 23—GERHARD TERBORCH THE YOUNGER: A Lady in an Interior. Gerard Terborch the Younger is the aristocratic figure of Dutch painting. He was brought up in a cultivated atmosphere that seemed to remain the setting of his own life and of those whom he depicted with such skill. His father was a painter and had visited Italy from 1602 to 1611. From about 1620 onwards he gave up painting as a profession and worked as a tax collector. Terborch senior instructed his children in drawing from the earliest possible age—drawings by Gerard exist from 1625. During the 1630's Terborch studied in Amsterdam and Haarlem, but did not settle down to a career of painting in the normal way. Instead, he began a long series of journeys abroad, visiting England, Italy, Spain, with only occasional stays in Holland. In 1646 he went to Münster in Westphalia where the great European peace conference was to take place. Though he remained for two or three years in Münster, he did not apparently do very much painting. Perhaps the commissions he anticipated did not materialise, or he may have been drawn into the realm of politics and diplomacy. However, from this period one great picture survives which is probably his finest group portrait. In 1648, Terborch painted the group of about sixty envoys and officials, representing Philip IV of Spain on the one hand and the Dutch on the other,

Plate 23. GERHARD TERBORCH THE YOUNGER (Zwolle 1617 - Deventer 1681):
A Lady in an Interior. Oil on panel, 39 x 27.5 cm (15½ x 11 ins). Dresden, Gemäldegalerie.

who concluded the final peace treaty between the two countries, the Peace of Münster. Terborch was very successful in giving characterisation even to such a large group. This *Group Portrait at Münster* (London, National Gallery) gives a lasting impression of Terborch's ability to capture the atmosphere and setting of a great occasion.

Yet the works which have made Terborch famous contrast in size and character with the Peace of Münster scene. In his early period, he was influenced by Duyster's style in the so-called barrack room scenes. His subjects and treatment soon became of a very different character, a development which must be partly explained by Metsu's influence. Terborch's interior scenes, with two or three figures, became the most refined in composition, rendering and sentiment, bringing this genre of painting to an unsurpassable quality. He was a gracious man, who moved easily among the most elevated society, with a sense of taste in every aspect of gracious living. His most important asset was an ability to bring the representation of any surface to a point of complete realism, that barely leaves us the slightest clue that it was painted with a brush controlled by a human hand. To this phenomenal sense of surface finish he added an equally refined sense of colour, although his use of colour was to some extent controlled by fashions in dress. His pure and gleaming colours are often seen against a monochrome background, and it is his feeling for light and shadow which gives a convincing atmosphere and spatial effect to the interiors. In the same way, his small full length portraits have a background and spatial setting which is suggested in the most subtle tonal differences. Though it is a disputed point, it seems certain that the style of these small portraits was influenced by his contact with Velazquez while in Spain.

The *Lady in an Interior* (Dresden, Gemäldegalerie) is one of his best known figures. This picture was probably painted as a preparation for works such as the *Paternal Admonition* (Berlin, Dahlem Museum). The silk dress is a typical masterpiece, where the iridescent oyster-silk has a mirror-like quality. Terborch's absorption with surface reality never prevented him from giving us a delicate hint of the secret thoughts of these actors in a world of trivial but delightful incident created by his own skill.

Plate 24—JAN STEEN: The Morning Toilet. The most universally popular Dutch artist was undoubtedly Jan Steen. His pictures in public galleries always seem to draw a group of delighted admirers, because Steen was blessed with an exceptional sense of humour of immediate and universal appeal. Perhaps the closest parallel to Steen in Dutch painting is Brouwer. Although Steen's technique is not derived from Brouwer, he possessed the same vitality of spirit as the older master. Both men led lives that were as gay and abandoned as many of their pictures. Steen, as an innkeeper, had a continual source of inspiration for his many representations of merry gatherings. In his earlier period he painted with considerable breadth and gusto, that eventually gave way to a rather tight and laboured method in his last years, when his forceful originality declined. Steen's reputation was marred by the very erratic nature of his large output. At his best, he was a draughtsman and painter of astonishing verve who could give his figures the fullest animation and invent highly original compositions. When Steen was painting in this vein, he did not need to pause over any problems, and his pictures have that sense of rhythm and spontaneity which reflect this fluent creative process.

One thinks of Steen as the painter of gay tavern groups, where manners and humour were coarser than those of today. By contrast, in his more intimate moments he could be a very refined and delightful artist, in a way that compares with Metsu. An example of this type is *The Morning Toilet* (Amsterdam, Rijksmuseum). Here Steen has captured, in a most unaffected way, a moment at the start of the day. The girl is smiling at some inner thought as she slowly pulls on her stocking. There is a slight discrepancy in the size of the slippers, which gives a rather naive charm to the foreground. Like many of his still-life details, the gleaming chamber-pot is skilfully painted. No matter how humble the details of everyday existence, they have their place in that overall study of simple, domestic life, which is one of the distinguishing features of the Dutch genre painters.

Plate 24. JAN STEEN (Leyden 1626 - 1679):
The Morning Toilet. Oil on panel, 37 x 28 cm (14½ x 10½ ins). Amsterdam, Rijksmuseum.